Dad Jokes

More Than 1000 Terribly Amusing Puns That Will Make You Laugh Out Loud!

Written by Harold Foster

Furthermore, the information that can be found within the pages described forthwith shall be considered both accurate and truthful when it comes to the recounting of facts. As such, any use, correct or incorrect, of the provided information will render the Publisher free of responsibility as to the actions taken outside of their direct purview. Regardless, there are zero scenarios where the original author or the Publisher can be deemed liable in any fashion for any damages or hardships that may result from any of the information discussed herein.

Additionally, the information in the following pages is intended only for informational purposes and should thus be thought of as universal. As befitting its nature, it is presented without assurance regarding its prolonged validity or interim quality. Trademarks that are mentioned are done without written consent and can in no way be considered an endorsement from the trademark holder.

Table of Contents

Introduction...5

Chapter 1: Funny Puns...10

Chapter 2: Questions and Answers- The Dad Version........... 48

Chapter 4: "Knock, Knock ... Who's There?"......................... 115

Chapter 5: Silly Stories...196

Bonus Chapter 1: Food Knock Knock Jokes........................ 225

Bonus Chapter: Riddles, Brain Teasers and Trick Questions for Kids... 247

Bonus Chapter 2: Easy Riddles 248

Conclusion 259

Introduction

You know it is coming. You are driving down the road, or you bring a new friend home for the first time, and your dad chimes in, "Hey, did you know..." Of course, those of you that know your dad immediately assume the "here we go again," look, but if there is an unsuspecting member of his audience, he has them hooked. And the gleam in his eye and sly smile is proof that something ridiculously embarrassing is coming. It is like he just cannot resist himself. He just has to make that corny joke.

But despite how many times you have heard your dad's jokes or how awful they are, you just cannot stop yourself from smiling, just a little bit, sometimes just to yourself so you do not egg him on. Most of the time, the jokes have been passed down from generation to generation. And part of the humor is not in the joke itself, but the way it is delivered. What makes a corny joke a dad joke is the delivery and the timing. And many, many repetitions of the same jokes. Now with the internet, the once only oral tradition of the dad joke has had a resurgence and a documentation like never before. Even comedians are embracing the rising popularity of the cringe-worthy comedy, imitating the timing and repetition for the amusement of their audiences.

Of course, these jokes are met with both unconditional love and annoyance. It carries a deep vein of intimate family bonds with the modern, superficiality of social media. This probably speaks to the current state of fatherhood and contemporary humor, but regardless of the "deep" meaning behind the enjoyment of dad jokes, these clean, harmless jokes garner pitying glances, slow groans and a few giggles. But what makes a joke a "dad joke?" Well, there are many variations. The classic joke or goofy story are always popular. But many have a theme of anti-humor, play on words, or just simply make no sense at all. Regardless of how it is phrased, if you time it right and use the right tone, you can easily make it a true dad joke. And of course, deliver the joke at an inappropriate or sensitive time, and you are sure to nail it. Think first meeting, graduation speech, during a menial fight....

No one really knows how dad jokes got their name and classification. It might have to do with childish humor, the desire to make your child smile, and pure exhaustion. It also is not confined to just the United States, many other cultures have a form of humor associated with generational, silly jokes. And yet, despite so many cultures continuing the tradition of gaff-worthy jokes, people continue to hate-love them. The content can be satirical and edgy. It can even be dark. But it can help current generations escape the heavy, nasty, stressful climate we live in. It offers the exact opposite, even just for a moment, so you can smile and keep going. You are enjoying the innocence and nostalgia of the "simpler" time. You can laugh with ease, no matter your education level or status.

As you begin to peruse the pages of this lovely, little book, you will find examples of dad jokes that you can read and memorize. Keep a few in your pocket for a rainy day and enjoy the groans and giggles you are sure to elicit the more you tell them. Remember, delivery is key! Below are some suggestions to help you tell the best dad joke of your life:

1. Be a dad. Especially a dad of young children. Think tired, worn out, and desperate to diffuse a situation with an irrational human. A mom can fill this description, too.

2. Take a deep breath and relax. You must be in the right frame of mind to pull off a corny joke. If you are too nervous or feeling awkward, the other person will, too. Dad jokes are best told in the moment, with a playful air about them. If you feel it, so will the other person.

3. Change your voice. Do not deliver a joke in one tone. Up and down and all around will make these jokes engage more people. Some folks do well with a deadpan, sarcastic one-liner, but most will do better if

you have some variety in the tone. Dad jokes are meant to be approachable for all ages and walks of life. Using fun voices, fast and slow speech, and high and low volume can do wonders for your delivery. And gestures! Make sure you add in some physical movements, too. Get your whole body into the story, and you are sure to deliver an awesome, cheesy joke.

4. Let people know that something is coming. A short pause and a playful twinkle in your eye will be sure to let your audience know something hilariously awful is about to happen. This little bit of suspense cues those who have fallen victim to your dad joke that they are about to get smothered in cheese. See what I did there.... A little pre-dad-joke humor for you....

5. If they do not crack a smile or offer a little scoff, walk away. Do not be desperate. That just always looks bad. They may be trying to save face in the situation and are secretly dying inside from laughter, but do not keep throwing your one-liner's at them in hopes of wearing them down. A single, well-played pun can cause lasting ripples of joy in those stone-faced maniacs. Trust you delivered a good one and walk away with your own laughter, even if you did not garner theirs.

6. Have confidence in the joke you are delivering. Do not try to tell a joke you do not really understand, do not have faith in its dad-ness, or do not feel will fit the

situation. Like at a funeral or when your mom is really, very mad at you. When you read the jokes in the following chapters, and it makes you laugh out loud, tuck those away to use for another day. Those are your bread-and-butter dad jokes for the future. This also helps with tip number five.

So, now that you know what a dad joke is and how to deliver it, it is time to start enjoying some dad jokes for yourself. Turn the page, get ready to crack a smile, and read these jokes in your cheesiest dad voice ever! Enjoy!

Chapter 1: Funny Puns

1. "I just watched a documentary about beavers. It was the best dam show I ever saw!"

2. "I would avoid that sushi if I was you. It is a little fishy!"

3. "You know, people say they picked their nose. I do not think I did, I was just born with mine!"

4. "There was a news report on the restaurant they opened on the moon. Apparently, the food is great, but the atmosphere is terrible!"

5. "I am not indecisive. Unless you want me to be...."

6. "If I had a dime for every book I finished reading, I would say, 'Well, is that not coincidental?'"

7. "I have a hard time with steak jokes. They are a rate medium well done."

8. "I can tell you how to tell the difference between a male and a female ant. They are all girls. Otherwise they would be uncles!"

9. "The fastest liquid on Earth is milk. It is pasteurized before you can see it!"

10. "I have been trying and trying to lose weight, but it somehow keeps finding me!"

11. "I love playing soccer. Not because I am good at it, but because of the kicks!"

12. "My first job I ever had was at a shoe recycling plant. Worst job ever. It destroyed soles!"

13. "If your nose smells and your feet run, do you think you are built upside down?"

14. "I tried to buy some camouflage pants the other days, but I could not find any anywhere!"

15. "I had a wild weekend. I went to this seafood disco. It was fun until I pulled a mussel!"

16. "I cut my finger while I was slicing cheese the other day. I think I may have grater problems."

17. "I had a nightmare last night that I was drowning in a sea of orange soda. It took me awhile to realize it was just a Fanta sea!"

18. "Life is pointless without geometry!"

19. "I gave all my dead batteries away, free of charge!"

20. "I am no comfortable taking the elevator. I take steps to avoid them!"

21. "A blue ship and a red ship crashed into one another the other day. Apparently all their passengers are marooned!"

22. "I wanted to go Hans free, so I deleted all the Germans I knew from my phone book!"

23. "I have been trying out the whiskey diet lately. It is working pretty well. I have lost three days already!"

24. "I bought my wife the new broom that came out a few months ago. Apparently it is sweeping the nation!"

25. "I donate to all the atheist organizations. They are all non-prophet!"

26. "I slept like a log last night. I do not recommend it. The fireplace is not comfortable."

27. "There was an arrest report in the paper today about a cop that caught two boys playing with fireworks and a car battery. Apparently, the cop charged one and let the other one off!"

28. "I got a new book the other day about the history of glue. It is awesome. I cannot put it down!"

29. "I saw a couple of peanuts walking down the street the other day. One was a salted."

30. "I started a new diet called the 'seafood diet.' It is very simple; I see food and then I eat it!"

31. "I should have stayed away from the seafood dish at the pancake house last night. Now I am feeling a little eel!"

32. "I started reading this book about anti-gravity. It is so good. It is impossible to put down!"

33. "I was so excited for Spring that I wet my plants!"

34. "I accidently bought my shoes from a drug dealer. I have no clue what they laced them with. I was tripping all day!"

35. "I lost my job at the factory today. You know, the calendar factory? Apparently, they did not like it when I took a few days off."

36. "There was a court show on television the other day where the judge was trying a case for a murder. The woman was charged with beating her husband to death

with a guitar. The judge asked her, 'first offender?' and she replied, 'No, first a Gibson, and then a Fender!"

37. "I had the weirdest dream last night that I was a car's muffler. I woke up this morning exhausted!"

38. "A new statistic shows that 5/4 of people are really bad with fractions!"

39. "Two guys walked into a bar. Thankfully the third one ducked!"

40. "You know, you really should not trust atoms. They make up everything!"

41. "I have the hardest time with the alphabet. I only know 25 letters. I do not know 'Y!'"

42. "Hey, look over at those cows! They truly are outstanding in their field!"

43. "I hate when the server asks, 'Soup or salad.' I do not want a Super Salad, I just want a regular one!"

44. "The knights of the round table always complained to King Arthur about Sir Cumference. He acquired his size from all the pi!"

45. "I was pulled into the police station for questioning yesterday. Apparently, someone stole a cheese sandwich. They really grilled me!"

46. "I saw two goldfish where in a tank the other day. I heard one of them say to the other, 'Do you know how to drive this thing?'"

47. "The reason the scarecrow got an award for being outstanding in his field? Hay, it is in his jeans!"

48. "I am exhausted today. I stayed up all night trying to figure out what happened to the sun. And then it dawned on me!"

49. "I swear I told you at least ten jokes to get you to laugh. Unfortunately, no pun in 10 did."

50. "I picked up a thesaurus the other day. It is the worst one I have ever seen. Not only is it awful, it is awful!"

51. "When your grandpa passed, he was peaceful and asleep. Thankfully not like the passengers in his car!"

52. "Sometimes when I am having a bad day I just tuck my knees in to my chest and lean forward. At least, that is how I roll."

53. "They all laughed when I told them that I was going to be a comedian. They are not laughing now!"

54. "I am serious; dad jokes are no laughing mater!"

55. "I told your sister that her eyebrows were drawn on too high. She looked so surprised!"

56. "In the park the other day I was watching some kids throw a frisbess, I wondered why it kept getting bigger. And then it hit me!"

57. "It is time to celebrate. I won my first cage fight! The other guy did not know what hit him!"

58. "I wanted to tell you a joke about fighting, but I forgot the punchline."

59. "I hope your mom does not realize I swapped out our bed for a trampoline. She will hit the ceiling!"

60. "I heard on the news today that the police were called to the daycare down the street. Turns out there were a bunch of kids there resisting a rest."

61. "Be careful opening up emails for the next few days. There is something going around about canned meat causing cancer. I am pretty sure it is just Spam."

62. "The police are all up in arms these days. Someone keeps stealing their patrol dogs. Thankfully they have several leads."

63. "Is it just me, or does pressing the F5 key seem refreshing?"

64. "This shovel sure is a groundbreaking invention."

65. "I am always having to separate facts from fiction. I hate being a librarian."

66. "When my wife told me I was not a flamingo I had to put my foot down."

67. "Did you know that when you go to the Weight Watchers website they make you disable the cookies?"

68. "I broke down and got a second job. I start at the restaurant tomorrow. I cannot wait."

69. "I have finally put the vacuum up for sale. It just collects dust around here."

70. "Tomorrow at the office it is Jamaican day. Everyone is dreading it."

71. "Back in the day it only cost $2 to adjust the air pressure in my tires. Now it costs $10! Well, I guess that is inflation for you."

72. "A strange salesman came to the door today. He was trying to sell me a coffin. I told him that is the last thing I need!"

73. "Beer is for thugs, tea is for mugs!"

74. "Your wedding was so beautiful. Not an eye was dry in the place. Even the cake was in tiers!"

75. "One cow was talking to the other in the pasture. The first cow turned to the other and asked, 'are you worried about mad cow disease?' The second cow replied, 'Not at all, I am a helicopter.'"

76. "A farmer was counting his cows in the field the other day. He counted only 196, but when he rounded them up, he had 200!"

77. "The paper had the obituary for the man that invented the throat lozenge. What is strange is that there will be no coffin at the funeral."

78. "I got a nasty bump on my head when a book fell on it this morning. I really only have my shelf to blame."

79. "On my way into work I farted in the elevator going up to my floor. It was wrong on so many levels!"

80. "The other night I was lying in bed, looking up at the stars, thinking …. 'where is my roof?'"

81. "I caught your grandpa pretending to be a gas station worker once. He was not fueling anyone!"

82. "I had surgery last month and the doctors had a few complications. They ended up removing everything on my left hand side. Now I am all right!"

83. "The other day I broke down and bought a quad bike. My dirt bike was just two tire-d."

84. "Whiteboards are a remarkable invention!"

85. "I have spent the last 98 days torturing this centipede. He is finally on his last legs now!"

86. "Darn it! I burnt the Hawaiian pizza. I should have put it on the aloha temperature!"

87. "I'm selling my broken guitar. No strings attached."

88. "An old college friend of mine accidently bit off his tongue once. He does not like to talk about it."

89. "I have built up quite a gun collection. I have been buying them from a guy that goes by the name 'T-Rex.' He is a small arms dealer."

90. "I was watching one of those court shows today and there was a guy who was guilt of damaging library books. He would use white out on all the punctuation. He said he was expecting a long sentence!"

91. "I bet it is tough being a plumber. They have to watch their life's work go down the drain."

92. "Make sure to give a shout out to your grandma. That is the only way she is going to hear you."

93. "As a math fanatic I have come to realize that there are ten types of people in this world; those that understand binary, and those that do no."

94. "You know, toaster's were the first pop-up notification."

95. "Every time I go to the grocery store I try to buy one of those divider things. But every time the lady behind the cash register puts it back!"

96. "I was reading a new book about Stockholm syndrome. At first I thought it was really bad, but by the time I finished I really liked it."

97. "If you really need a job the moisturizer factory is hiring. The best advice I have heard is to make sure to apply daily."

98. "When I took that job at the travel agency I really thought I would go places."

99. "I got so angry the other day when I could not find my stress ball."

100.   "I had to go to the hospital the other day for a broken arm. I told the doctor I had broken it in several places. The doctor replied, 'Well, do not go to those places!'"

101,   "I was watching a movie about a war the other day and one of the privates ran up to a commander and was saying, 'General! General! The troops are revolting!' The general looked at the private and said, 'Well, you are pretty repulsive yourself.'"

102.   "If the phone rings and it is for me, do not answer it!"

103.   "I grabbed a pair of those complimentary headphones on my way to the airplane but when I put

them on they did not say one nice thing about me. I always seem to get the broken pairs!"

104.   "I saw a wino eating grapes the other day. They seemed to get a little upset when I told them that had to wait."

105.   "At first I was shocked when the highway police called me to say you were a thief, but when I got home, all the signs were there."

106.   "I wanted to figure out who loved me more, so I put both your mom and the dog into the trunk of the car. I figure, when I open the trunk, I will see who is happy to see me!"

107.   "I'm planning on living on forever. So far, so good!"

108.   "One of our cows had a calf today! Now she is de-calf-inated!"

109.   "One day you are the best thing since sliced bread, and the next, you are toast!"

110.   "Why do penguins not fly? They are not tall enough to be a pilot."

111.   "What is the name of the woman who stands in between two goal posts? Annette."

112.   "All money is tainted. That is the problem. It taints mine and it taint yours."

113.   "When a clock gets really hungry it goes back four seconds."

114.   "Your mom broke into song when she could not find the key."

115.   "Have you ever wondered who answers the phones at the Keebler elves' office? I heard it is a tree-ceptionist."

116.   "The marathon runner I was watching on TV clearly had on shoes that did not fit him right. He said he was suffering the agony of da feet."

117.   "How would you define a Will? It is a Dead Giveaway."

118.   "Your debt will stay with you if you cannot budge it."

119.   "Your sister was dating a guy with a wooden leg but it broke off."

120.   "What do you have to know in order to be a successful auctioneer? Lots."

121.   "The calendar's days are numbered."

122.   "What do you call a train carrying a load of toffee? A chew chew train!"

123.   "Have you heard about the most popular wine in the world? *In a whining voice* I do not like Brussels sprouts!"

124.   "Have you heard about how Chickens dance? Chick to chick."

125.   "On what tree do fingers grow? A palm tree!"

126.   "A Mexican fireman just had twin sons. He named them Hose A and Hose B."

127.   "What is the name of the country where they all drive red cars? Red carnation."

128.   "The news reported an incident at the upholstery factory. Apparently, a mane fell in. They said he is expected to be fully recovered."

129.   "I hate when I have a Freudian slip. I always say one thing but mean your mother."

130.   "A hangover is really you just suffering the wrath of grapes."

131.   "What did the grape say when the elephant stepped on it? Not much, it just let out a little wine."

132.   "Captains of the sea do not like crew cuts."

133.   "When I talk about Pavlov, does the name ring a bell?"

134.   "The only way to be successful in a diet is to have mind over platter."

135.   "A gossip girl is a woman who has a great sense of rumor."

136.   "When you sunbathe and read at the same time it will make you well, red."

137.   "In a manor of speaking, a man's home is his castle."

138.　　"Honey, can you pass the Dijon vu? It is the same mustard like before."

139.　　"It is an I for an I whenever two egotists meet."

140.　　"A poet who is backwards will always write in verse."

141.　　"Your vote counts in democracy. Your count votes in feudalism."

142.　　"It is poultry in motion when the chicken crosses the road."

143.　　"If you do not pay the priest who performed your exorcism will you get repossessed?"

144.　　"The best two things a lady gets when she gets married is a new name and a dress."

145.　　"If you can show me a piano that is falling down a mineshaft, I will show you a flat miner."

146.   "Each morning is the dawn of a new error."

147.   "If you throw a grenade into a French kitchen you will make linoleum blown apart."

148.   "Having a boiled egg in the morning is hard to beat."

149.   "You know you have a photogenic memory. You just have never developed it."

150.   "Once you have seen one shopping center you have seen a mall."

151.   "If a person jumps off the Paris Bridge they are in Seine."

152.   "The first time that actress saw a grey hair when preparing for her role, she thought she would dye."

153.   "I was lucky to get that recipe from the baker the other day. They only trade their secrets on a knead-to-know basis."

154.   "The North Pole elves are subordinate clauses."

155.   "The acupuncture I got the other day was a jab well done."

156.   "I heard about this Buddhist monk who refused Novocain during his root canal the other day. Apparently he wanted to transcend dental medication."

157.   "Shotgun weddings are a case of wife or death."

158.   "Time flies like an arrow. Fruit flies like a banana."

159.   "Do you dream in color? They say that is just a pigment of your imagination."

160.   "A new business in Australia opened up recently. They put up a pretty exciting sign for their networking business. It said, 'The LAN Down Under!'"

161.   "When your mother told me I was just average, I told her she was just being mean."

162.   "The blood type of a pessimist is always B-."

163.   "A couple of months before your uncle passed he asked me to cover his back with lard. After that, he really went down hill fast!"

164.   "Did you know that the first computer was dated back to Adam and Eve's time? It was an Apple with limited memory. It was just one byte. Everything crashed."

165.   "The nurse told the doctor today, 'Doctor, the patient one line one is saying that they are invisible. Can you speak with them or would you like me to schedule an appointment?' The doctor replied, 'Today is pretty busy. Tell him I cannot see him right now.'"

166.   "Son, I want to thank you for finally explaining the word 'many' to me. It really means a lot."

167.   "Your mother told me that she is going to leave me. She said it is because I keep pretending to be a transformer. I told her she cannot leave, I can change!"

168.   "Your grandpa kept telling us to be positive when we went to see him in the hospital before he died. It is hard to go one without him. It was so unfortunate no one could remember his blood type."

169.   "I do not understand the draw for eBay. I wanted to buy a new lighter but all they had were 15,238 matches."

170.   "The bar down the street changed from beer nuts to deer nuts. Before, the beer nuts cost about $2.50. Now the deer nuts are under a buck!"

171.   "I saw an ad in today's paper for a burial plot. I thought to myself, 'Well, that is the last thing I need!'"

172.   "It is more productive to think outside of the box when you suffer from claustrophobia."

173. "I have some news to share. I just burned 3,000 calories. Honestly, that is the last time I leave brownies cooking in the oven while I lay down for my afternoon nap."

174. "I was once addicted to the Hockey Pokey. Thank God I turned myself around!"

175. "What is it called when a dictionary is doing drugs? High-Definition!"

176. "Do you know the reason why atheists do not attempt to solve exponential equations? The do not believe in higher powers!"

177. "The weirdest things happened today. The cops came by to tell me that the dogs were chasing kids on bikes. I told them that was impossible. My dogs do not even own bikes!"

178. "I would like to tell the mathematician who invented the number zero, "Thanks for nothing!"

179.   "While we were travelling in Mexico this summer we watched a street magician. He said, 'Uno, dose...' and then, poof! He disappeared without a trace!"

180.   "I had to return my new gloves today. Turns out they were both lefts. On the one hand, it was great, but on the other, it was just not right."

181.   "I used to suffer from an addiction to soap. Thank God I am clean now!"

182.   "E.T.'s mom made a cameo in the sequel. The first thing she says to him was, 'E.T., where on Earth have you been?'"

183.   "Your mom is pretty made at me today. I handed her a glue stick instead of a chap stick. She still is not talking to me!"

184.   "Today I ordered 2,000 pounds of soup from the Chinese restaurant down the street. It was Won Ton."

185.   "Did you know that Oxygen is actually a toxic gas? Turns out that any person that inhales it will die in about 80 years!"

186.   "I was originally going to be the first recipient for a brain transplant, but I ended up changing my mind."

187.   "An artist was arrested in a courtroom today. I wish I knew more but the details are pretty sketchy."

188.   "Whatever you do, do not spell 'part' backwards. It is a trap!"

189.   "The doctor told me not to worry about the bird flu epidemic. Turns out it is tweetable."

190.   "Your mom told me the other day she wanted to split up. She hates that I double as a private investigator. I told her it was a good idea. That way we can cover more ground that way."

191. "I picked up a 'Get Better Soon' card the other day. No, she is not sick, but I do think she could get better."

192. "How did I avoid Iraq? Iran!"

193. "I wanted to tell you a joke about chemistry, but I know it will not get a good reaction."

194. "A piece of advice: Never engage in mental combat with those that are unequipped."

195. "If four out of five suffer from diarrhea, does that mean that the fifth actually enjoys it?"

196. "For Halloween this year your mom and I are going to dress up as peanuts. That way everyone will be able to tell how nuts we are!"

197. "Two blondes set off driving to Disney World. On their way they saw a sign that said, 'Disney World Left.' They turned around and went home, crying all the way."

198. "I have decided to write a song. It is going to be about tortillas. You know, it is going to be more of a rap."

199. "I came up with a few jokes about unemployed people the other day. They are not any good. None of them work."

200. "Your mom has been asking for me to blow on her when she gets one of her hot flashes. But honestly, I am not a fan."

201. "It is a good thing I know sign language. It has come in pretty handy."

202. "I got kicked out of the football game and was told that my actions were banned at all local sporting events. Turns out they made doing the 'Wave' illegal. Too many blondes kept drowning."

203.   "My boss wanted to fire me the other day. He said I was bullying other people in the workplace. Do not worry. I stared him down until he apologized."

204.   "The other day in the woods while I was hunting I saw the longest rock ever. When I measured it, it was 1,760 yards long! It must be some sort of milestone, or something."

205.   "We got robbed the other day. They took everything, but left soap, towels, shower gel, and deodorant. Dirty, no goo thieves."

206.   "I am an emotionally constipated mess. It has been several days since I gave a crap."

207.   "The paper had a write up about the arrest of the world's best tongue twister. Apparently, they are predicting he will get a tough sentence."

208.   "At the doctor's office that I go to they always have two doctors' available at all times. They consider it a paradox."

209.   "It is shocking to people how bad I am as an electrician."

210.   "This clown opened the door for me this morning. I thought to myself, 'Well, that is a nice jester.'"

211.   "I cannot stand peer pressure. And you know what, you should, too."

212.   "My friend Bill tried to get me with a couple of bird puns the other day. I told him that toucan play that game!"

213.   "I got canned from my job at the orange juice factory. I just could not concentrate."

214.   "Your teacher once asked you in a Parent-Teacher conference if you were ignorant or apathetic. You told her, 'I do not know and do not care.'"

215.   "You know why justice is a dish best served cold? Because if it was served warm it would be just water."

216.   "I am home early because my boss told me to have a good day. I took him up on his suggestion."

217.   "My mechanic's shop got a new mechanic. He is Korean. I cannot understand a word he says. He talks with such a heavy Hyundai Accent."

218.   "I got fitted for a neck brace a year or so ago. Ever since then I have not looked back."

219.   "In my psychiatrist appointment the other day the doctor told me I was too preoccupied with getting vengeance. I told him we would see about that!"

220.   "Some darn thieves stole my toilet! The police have nothing to go on now!"

221.   "I felt trapped forever in the Apple store, so I went to the bathroom to escape. It did not work; there are no Windows."

222. "During our weekly poker game, I ended up running out of chips. I used dried fruit and almonds instead. Everyone went nuts when I started raisin the stakes!"

223. "I always dreamed of marrying an archaeologist. I figured, the older I would get, the more interested she would become!"

224. "My boss put out a memo the other day that he was going to fire the person in the office with the worst posture. I have a big hunch that it is going to be me."

225. "Did you know that I had a job for a short time as a lumberjack? I could not hack it though so they gave me the ax."

226. "I relish the fact that you have mustard the strength to ketchup with me."

227. "I used to be a banker, but I ended up losing interest."

228.   "I had the hardest time remembering how to throw a boomerang. Thankfully it eventually came back to me."

229.   "I wanted to tell you a joke about sodium, but then I decided, 'NA.'"

230.   "I hate that people do not get my puns. They think they are so funny."

231.   "You know, I was thinking; If a bus station is where busses stop, and a train station is where trains stop, what should happen at my work station?"

232.   "I went out and bought a new dictionary the other day. When I got it home I realized that the pages were actually blank. I have no words for how upset I am."

233.   "I tried to put the moves on this philosophy instructor of mine once. Unfortunately, she never knew if I existed or not."

234.   "I had a job when your mom and I first got together in the sausage factory. I ended up quitting. I could not make ends meet."

235.   "Since the right-hand side of the brain controls the left side of your body, this means that only lefties are the people in their right mind."

236.   "My doctor told me the other day to quit using Q-tips all the time. Honestly, it went in one ear and right out the other."

237.   "I can hardly see myself cleaning mirrors."

238.   "This new book I got is written in braille. Something bad is about to happen in the story. I know because I can just feel it!"

239.   "Your mom is so depressed. It has been raining for three days with no break. She is just standing at the window, looking through. It is so sad. You know, if the rain does not stop tomorrow I am going to have to let her in."

240.   "I tried watching the Neverending Story. I just could not finish it though."

241.   "Insect puns are the worst. They really bug me!"

242.   "Like Uncle Ben said to Spiderman, 'With great reflexes comes great response ability.' Or something like that."

243.   "There is no better time to open a gift than the present."

244.   "Hacker's tried to ruin my online business the other day. I was able to preserve the website, and that is really domain thing."

245.   "Your grandfather was there for the Titanic. He tried to warn them. He said he screamed and shouted about the ice burg coming. No one did anything about the ship, but they did throw him out of the theater."

246.   "When I was young I felt like I was a man trapped in a female's body. Then I was born!"

247.   "It is so hard to explain puns to kleptomaniacs. They are always taking things literally."

248.   "A nudist colony discovered a hole in one of their walls. The police are looking into it."

249.   "I hung up a picture on the wall a few days ago. I nailed it."

250.   "This guy in line the other day was a pain in the butt. I was going to give him a nasty look, but he already had one."

251.   "I used to work for a factory that made fire hydrants. Unfortunately, there was nowhere to park near the place."

Chapter 2: Questions and Answers-The Dad Version

1. "What do you call a Mexican who has lost his car?" Carlos!

2. "What do you call a fake noodle?" An Impasta!

3. "What is brown and sticky?" A stick!

4. "Why did the cookie cry?" Because her dad was a WAFER for so many days!

5. "What did the mountain climber name his son?" Cliff

6. "How many apples grow on a tree?" All of them!

7. "How does a penguin build their house?" Igloos it.

8. ""Why do you never see elephants hiding in a tree?" They're too good at it!

9. "Where does a one-legged server work?" IHOP

10. "Why does a bike rest on its leg?" Because it got two tired!

11. "What did one snowman say to the other?" Does it smell like carrots to you?

12. "How can you make a tissue dance?" You put a boogie in it!

13. "Why was the blonde staring at the orange juice?" The carton said concentrate!

14. "What is the best way to plan a space party?" You planet!

15. "What do you call a belt with a watch on it?" A waist of time!

16. "What is a thief's shoe of choice?" Sneakers!

17. "Do you know what happened to the man charged with stealing a calendar?" He got 12 months!

18. "Where can you find a bulk order of vegetable broth?" The stock market!

19. "What is the name of the man who's laying by your font door?" Matt

20. "What is a fishes name that does not have any eyes?" Fsshh

21. "What is the name of the man that has only a nose-less head?" Nobody nose!

22. "What do you call the man that has a rubber to?" Roberto

23. "Why wont lobsters donate to charity?" they are shellfish!

24. "What does the ocean say to the beach?" Nothing at all, it just waves!

25. "Why is living in Switzerland such a positive experience?" The flag is a big big plus!

26. "Why do octopus always beat a shark in a fight?" They are well armed!

27. "What did the poppa spider say to the little spider?" You spend all your time on the web!

28. "How much does a hipster weigh?" An Instagram!

29. "What do you call a bunch of killer wales playing classical instruments?" An Orca-stra!

30. "Why did they disqualify the large cat from the game?" It was a Cheetah!

31. "How do you make holy water?" You have to boil the hell out of it!

32. "Why did the Clydesdale give the Shetland pony a drink of water?" Because it was a little horse!

33. "What is one cheese that you can never have?" Nacho cheese!

34. "What did the big tomato say to the baby tomato?" Ketchup!

35. "What do they call 50 Cent in Zimbabwe?" 400 Million!

36. "What did the little corn say to the mama corn?" Where is popcorn?

37. "What do you call a legless cow?" Ground beef!

38. "What did the daddy buffalo say to his little boy when he dropped him off at school?" Bison!

39. "Why was the scarecrow recognized for his achievements?" Because he is outstanding in his field!

40. "Why did someone spread peanut butter all over the highway?" To compliment the traffic jam!

41. "Why are chicken coups only allowed to have two doors?" Otherwise they would be a chicken sedan!

42. "Why are seagulls not allowed to fly over the bay?" Because otherwise they would be called bagels!

43. "What should you do if a blonde ever throws a grenade at you?" Pull out the pin and toss it back to her!

44. "Where does Batman go when he needs to pee?" To the Batroom!

45. "Can you name the one difference between an Indian elephant and an African elephant?" 5,000 miles!

46. "What do you call a legless sheep?" A cloud!

47. "What did zero say to the number eight?" Nice belt!

48. "Why are skeletons always so chill?" Nothing can get under their skin!

49. "Did you hear about the fires at the circus?" It was in tents!

50. "Why must scuba divers fall backwards out of the boat into the water?: If they fell forwards they would fall onto the deck of the boat!

51. "Have you heard about the new band, cellophane?" They are mostly wrap.

52. "What kind of religion do cows practice?" Moodoo!

53. "Why is Superman always invited to dinner parties?" He   is   a   supper-hero!

54. "What is an annoying pepper always up to?" Getting jalapeno face!

55. "What time is your dentist appointment?" Tooth hurty!

56. "Why did the owl skip the funeral service for the rabbit?" He is just not good with mourning.

57. "Did you know that French fries are not cooked in France?" They are cooked in Greece!

58. "How did the hacker know the password to Forest Gump's account?" It was one, Forest, one.

59. "What do they say about the inventor of the lifesaver?" That he made a mint!

60. "How do they label a factory that sells products that pass inspection?" Satisfactory!

61. "Did you know that the cemetery here is the most popular place in town?" Everyone is dying to get there!

62. "Why did the invisible man get rejected after the interview?" They could not see him doing the job!

63. "Did you hear that Fed Ex and UPS are merging for the holidays?" They are going to be called Fed-up!

64. "What was Beethoven's favorite fruit?" Ba-na-na-na!

65. "What did the stallion yell after it tripped?" Help! I have fallen and I cannot giddy up!

66. "What is the name of a cow that only has two legs?" Lean beef

67. "What happens when a rhino and an elephant have a baby?" Eleph-ino

68. "How many times do you need to tickle an octopus to make it laugh?" Ten tickles!

69. "How does one prisoner talk to the others in jail?" Cell phones!

70. "Why does the bike keep falling over?" It was two-tired!

71. "What do you call a magical dog?" Labracadabrador!

72. "Why do vampires stay away from Taylor Swift?" She has bad blood!

73. "Did you hear the news about the ban on round hay bails in Kansas?" Cows were not getting their square

meal!

74. "What is the name of the fish with two knees?" Two-knee   fish!

75. "What pet should you avoid if you do not want something   that   makes   noise?"   Trum-pet!

76. "What happens when a snowman and a vampire get together?"   Frostbite!

77. "What do you call a deer that has no eyes?" No i-deer!

78. "What happens when cheese gets lonely?" It is provolone!

79. "What does a zombie eat when it is a vegetarian?" Ggggrrrraaaaiiinnnss!

80. "Why do people always have a problem when they buy Velcro?"   It   is   such   a   rip   off!

81. "Where did the vampires in college always shop for clothes?" Forever 21

82. "Have you heard the new band 1023 megabytes?" They are pretty good but they till have not gotten a gig yet!

83. "Why did the singer always bring a bucket with her on stage?" To carry her tune!

84. "What is the name of a boomerang that does not come back to you?" A stick

85. "Why were people planning a funeral celebration for hot water?" They knew it will be mist!

86. "What happens when your iPhone and iPad fall into the bathtub filled with water?" They sync.

87. "Can February, March?" No, but April, May!

88. "How many South Americans does it take to change a light bulb?" A Brazilian!

89. "What is the dumbest animal in the world?" A polar bear.

90. "What cheese is made backwards?" Edam!

91. "Why do chickens have to sit on their eggs?" They cannot sit on chairs!

92. "Why do flamingos stand on one of their legs?" So they do not fall over!

93. "Did you hear about the kidnapping a the school today?" It ended up ok, the teacher woke him up!

94. "What happens when you cross the Atlantic with the Titanic?" You get about halfway.

95. "Why are the French fans of eating snails?" They do not like to eat fast food!

96. "What is the greatest nation in the world?" Donation! Fork over $!oo!

97. "What is white and cannot climb up trees?" A Freezer!

98. "What is red and really bad for your teeth?" A brick!

99. "What is red and smells like blue paint?" Red paint!

100. "What is the difference between a fly and a bird?" A bird can fly but a fly cannot bird!

101.   "What did George Washington say after crossing the Delaware River?" It is time o get out of the boat.

102.   "What happens when a frog parks illegally?" It gets toad!

103.   "Did you hear the news about the cheese factory explosion in France?" All that remained was de-Brie!

104.   "Why did Shakespeare's wife leave him?" She could not handle any more of the dramas!

105.   "Why should you never trust stairs?" They are always   up   to   something!

106.   "Why should you ride in an elevator when you are sad?" They will always lift you up!

107.   "What do you call a short psychic who broke out of   jail?"   A   small   medium   at   large!

108.   "How can you tell when a blonde tried to send an email?" She stuffed th disk drive full of envelopes!

109.   "What is the name of a queue of rabbits that are only jumping backwards?" A receding hairline!

110.   "What kind of horse sleeps during the day and only comes out at night?" A night-mare!

111.   "What happens is you sing a country song backwards?" You get your wife and job back!

112.   "What happens when a farmer pampers his cows?" You get spoiled milk!

113.   "Why are gorillas nostrils so big?" They have big fingers!

114.   "What happens when you cross a highway with a bike?" Run over!

115.   "What did the Buddhist monk order at the Chicago hotdog stand?" Make me one with everything!

116.   "Where does the General keep his armies?" In his sleevies!

117.   "Why are koala bears not considered bears" They did   not   meet   the   koala-fications!

118.   "What do you call bears that have no ears?" B

119.   "What happens to a man who is agnostic, an insomniac, and is dyslexic?" He lays awake all night wondering if there is a dog!

120.   "What is a foot long and slippery?" A slipper!

121.   "What did one soldier say to the other when they were in a tank?" Blub, blub, blub, blub!

122.   "How did I know what happened when a vegan, atheist, and crossfitter walked into a bar?" They could not stop talking about it!

123.   "How Long is a Chinese name." Yes, it really is!

124.   "What is a pirate's favorite letter of the alphabet?" You would think it was "R," but it is really the "C!"

125.   "Have you heard the latest about these corduroy pillows?" They are making plenty of headlines!

126.   "What did the green grape tell the purple grape?" It's ok, friend! Breathe! Breathe!

127.   "What is the similarity between Winnie the Pooh and Alexander the Great?" They both have the same middle   name!

128.   "What did the right eye say to the left?" Between you and me, something sure does smell!

129.   "What happens when two cannon balls get married?"   They   make   bb's!

130   "Why did the cowboy get a Daschund?" He wanted   to   get   a   long   little   doggie!

131.   "Have you heard the catch to Cole's Law?" Thinly   sliced   cabbage!

132.   "What happened when the invisible woman married the invisible man?" Their kids were nothing to look   at,   either!

133.   "Did you see the cat laying on the ground over there?" It must not be feline well.

134.   "Did you hear they arrested the energizer bunny the other day? He was charged with battery!"

135.   "What happens when you see a crime committed at an Apple store?" You are considered an iWitness!

136.   "What is red and goes up and down?" a tomato riding in an elevator!

137.   "What is green, fuzzy, and will kill you if it falls out of a tree?" A pool table!

138.   "Did you head about the Italian chef that died the other day?" He pasta away.

139.   "What a more useful invention that the first telephone?" The second telephone!

140.   "What do you call two women paddling in a canoe?" Ky — yakkers!

141.   "Do you know what your grandpa said before he kicked the bucket?" He sad, 'I wonder how far I can

kick   this   bucket!"

142.   "Did you hear about the court case between the man and the airline?" He went after them when his luggage went missing. He lost the case.

143.   "Do you know why you should never criticize someone until you have walked a mile in their shoes?" Because that way you are a mile away and have their shoes   when   you   criticize   them!

144.   "What do you call the security guards that watches over the Samsung store?" Guardians of the Galaxy!

145.   "Can you explain the difference between a nicely dressed man on a bicycle and a poorly dressed man on a tricycle?" A tire!

146.   "What do you call a priest that quits and then becomes a lawyer?" A father in law!

147.   "Did you hear about the kid that got hit in the head with a soda" He lucked out. Thankfully it was a soft   drink!

148. "Why was Cinderella kicked off the soccer team?" She was the only one to run away from the ball!

149. "What do you call a motorcycle that laughs?" Yamahahaha.

150. "Why did the teacher with crossed eyes end up losing her job?" She had no control over her pupils.

151. "Why does the leopard never play hide and seek?" It is always spotted!

152. "Did you see the advertisement for the newest reversible jacket?" I cannot wait to see how it turns out.

153. "Why do aliens avoid coming to our planet?" It has awful ratings. It only has one star!

154. "How was Jesus able to save the world when he was crucified?" Only because he nailed it!

155. "Why did the scientist remove his doorbell and install a door knocker instead?" He wanted to win the Nobel prize!

156.   "Did you hear about the two silk worms that were in a race?" It ended in a tie.

157.   "What do you call a cow with a twitch?" Beef Jerky!

158.   "What do you call a cow during an earthquake?" Milk-shake!

159.   "Why are spiders so good at playing tennis?" They have a great topspin!

160.   "How do you know if your computer has the Miley virus?" It stops twerking.

161.   "Why was the picture sentenced to life in jail?" It was framed!

162.   "Why did the bee get married?" He found his honey!

163.   "Why should you get a universal remote?" It changes everything!

164.   "What do you call a person that is afraid of Santa Clause?"   Clause-   trophobic.

165.   "What was the name of the Asian pilot that crashed that plane the other day?" Sum Ting Wen Wong.

166.   "How do trees access the Internet?" They log in!

167.   "What kind of under garments do clouds wear?" Thunderwear!

168.   "What will happen to you if you eat shoe polish and   yeast?"   You   will   rise   and   shine!

169.   "Did you hear about the math teacher that was afraid of negative numbers?" He would stop at nothing to avoid them!

170.   "Can a kangaroo jump higher than the Empire State building?" Of course! The Empire State building cannot   jump!

171.   "Why does Snoop Dog always carry an umbrella with   him?"   Fo   Drizzle!

172.   "Where do sheep go to get their hair cut?" A Baaaaaa   Baaaaaa   shop!

173.   "What does the little fish say when they run into the big wall?" Dam!

174.   "What is the last thing that goes through a bug's mind when they hit your windshield?" His butt!

175.   "What goes, 'Haha! Thump!'?" A man who laughed   his   head   off!

176.   "Why in the world are pirate's so mean?" I have no   idea,   they   just   'R'!

177.   "Have you heard about the cannibal that passed his   brother   in   the   woods?"

178.   "What happens when you place a candle inside a suit   of   armor?"   A   Knight   light!

179.   "What do you call a nun that sleep walks?" A roamin' catholic!

180.   "What happens when a couple of drums and a cymbal falls off a cliff?" Ba-dum Tish

181.   "Why did the orange finally stop?" It ran out of juice.

182.   "Why is six so scared of seven?" Because seven eight nine.

183.   "Why did that stop light turn red?" Well, you would too if you had to change in the middle of the intersection!

184.   "What do you do with a chemist who dies?" You barium.

185.   "What did the farmer say when he could not find his   tractor?" Where is my tractor?

186.   "What does the man in the moon do when his hair   is   grown   out?" Eclipse it!

187.   "Why did the coffee cup file a police report?" Because   it   got   mugged.

188. "What do you call an elephant that is not important?" An irrelephant!

189. "Why is it easy to weigh a fish?" Because it has its own scales.

190. "Want me to tell you a joke about construction?" Sorry, I am still working on it.

191. "What do you call a psychic that has put on a lot of weight?" A four chin teller.

192. "You know what really makes my day?" The rotation of the Earth!

193. "Are you thinking about going on that all almond diet?" I think that is just nuts!

194. "Why does Peter Pan always have to fly?" He never lands!

195. "Why do blind people never go skydiving?" It scares the crap out of their dogs.

196. "Why did the old man fall into the well in his backyard?" He could not see that well.

197.   "How long does it take to eat a clock?" I have no idea,   but   it   is   very   time   consuming!

198.   "What do you call a French man who wears sandals?"   Phillipe   Phillope.

199.   "What is orange and sounds like a parrot?" Carrot

200.   "Where do you find cows that have no legs?" Right   were   you   left   them.

201.   "Does a deaf person think a person yawning is actually   screaming?"

202.   "How do crazy people make their way through a forest?" The take the psycho path.

203.   "What did the light say to the sports car?" Do not look at me! I am about the change!

204.   "What did one hat say to the other?" You stay here.   I   will   go   on   ahead.

205.   "Why did the shrimp not want to share its special treasure?" He is a little shellfish!

206.   "Why did the blonde eat her makeup?" She wanted to be pretty on the inside, too.

207.   "What kinds of people do banks lend money to?" The kinds of people that can prove that they do not need   it!

208.   "What is one of the easiest ways to prove to yourself that someone cares?" Miss a couple payments.

209.   "How can you make sure that at least one person is listening to you?" Talk to yourself!

210.   "How can you live a balanced life?" Hold a cupcake   in   both   hands.

211.   "Who stole my Microsoft Office?" I will find you. You   have   my   Word!

212.   "Why was there a baguette trapped in a cage at the zoo?" The zookeeper said it was bread in captivity!

213. "What do you call a Wall Street alligator?" An invest -i- gator!

214. "What is the city in Nevada that only allows dentists to live there?" Floss Vegas!

215. "What looks like half an apple?" The other half of the apple.

216. "Do I like telling dad jokes?" Only when he laughs!

217. "What did one vowel say after another vowel saved his life?" Aye E, I Owe you.

218. "Did you hear that rumor about butter?" If not, I am not going to be the one to spread it.

219. "What do you call a man that tells dad jokes but is not a dad?" A faux pa!

220. "Why it is impossible to send a telegram to Washington today?" Because Washington is dead!

221. "Do you challenge me to clear the table?" Give me a running start and I bet I can make it!

222.   "Why did your uncle name his dogs Rolex and Timex?" He wanted them to be his watch dogs.

223.   "Did you know that the difference between a numerator and denominator is a short line?" Do not worry. Only a fraction of people actually understand that!

224.   "How do you drop an egg onto a concrete floor and avoid breaking it?" Well, a concrete floor is pretty hard   to   break!

225.   "If ten men can build a wall in eight hours, how long will it take five men to build it?" No time at all. It is   already   built!

226.   "About how many birthdays does a Chinese woman   have?"   One,   like   everyone   else!

227.   "If you had three apples and four oranges in one hand and four apples and three oranges in the other hand,   what   would   you   have?   "   Huge   hands!

228.   "How can you lift an elephant with one hand?" Do not worry about it. You will never find an elephant

that   has   one   hand.

229.   "How can a man go eight days without sleep?"
He   sleeps   at   night.

230.   "What often falls but never gets hurt?" Snow

231.   "What is that no man ever saw which never was
but   always   will   be?"   Tomorrow

232.   "What can you never eat for breakfast?" Dinner!

233.   "What three letters change a girl into a
woman?" A-G-E

234.   "What happened when the wheel was invented?"
It   started   a   revolution.

235.   "Why do most married men die before their
wives?"   They   wanted   to.

236.   "What do diapers and Politicians have in
common?" You have to change both of them often, for
the   exact   same   reasons!

237.   "What is the definition of the early evening news?" It must start with the greeting, "Good evening," and then spend the rest of the time explaining why it actually   is   not   a   good   one."

238.   "What device will find furniture in a poorly lit room   every   time?"   Your   shins.

239.   "Why do parents give children a middle name?" So it is very obvious when they are big trouble.

240.   "If you throw a red stone into the blue sea what it   will   become?"   Wet!

241.   "What did the cowboy say went he went into the car showroom in Germany?" Audi.

242.   "What is the quickest way to speed up your 70 year old Mother's heart rate?" Tell her she is pregnant.

243.   "What is the best way to avoid wrinkles as you age?"   Take   off   your   glasses.

244.   "How you know that you are flying with a 'no frills' airline?" You need the exact change to board.

245.   "Why do 'no frills' airlines never show movies on their flights?" They do not have to. You are too busy watching your life flash before your eyes the whole time.

246.   "On a turkey, which side would you find most feathers?" Outside.

247.   "What gets wet while drying?" A towel

248.   "Why is it that all cats dislike flying saucers?" It frustrates them that they cannot reach the milk.

249.   "What animal has more lives than the cat, who has nine lives?" A frog. It croaks everyday.

250.   "Which ballet does pigs like best?" Swine Lake.

251.   "What is the biggest difference between chopped pork and pea soup?" Every person can chop pork, but not every person can pee soup.

252.   "Why is it that we do not eat clowns?" They taste too   funny.

253. "If you saw two cowboys in a kitchen, which would be the real one?" The one standing by the range.

254. "Where would you find a dog with one leg?" In the same spot you had left it at.

255. "What shakes and twitches and can be found at the bottom of the sea?" A nervous wreck!

256. "Why did the room that was packed with married people seem empty?" There was not single person there.

257. "What's the difference between a pessimist and a magnet?" At least the magnet has a positive side!

258. "What is the longest sentence that a man knows?" I do.

259. "What is a quicker way to transfer money than electronic banking?" Marriage.

260. "What would you have if you crossed a panther with a beef burger?" Incredibly fast food!

261.   "What would you have if you crossed a pig with a karate expert?" Pork chop!

262.   "Why do traffic lights rarely go swimming?" It takes them too much time to change.

263.   "Why do thieves shower before they commit a crime?" They want to have a clean getaway.

264.   " What type of bow can never be tied?" A Rainbow!

265.   "Why did Jack take a prune out for the evening?" He struggled getting a date.

266.   "What do you call an infant monkey?" A chimp off the ol' block!

267.   "Why was the pirate not allowed to play poker?" He always sat on the deck.

268.   "Which is the loudest state in America?" Illi-Noise!

269.   "Why is it that birds fly southwards for the winter?" you try walking that far every year!

270.   "Why is it unpleasant to eat a meal next to a group of basketball players?" They dribble way too often!

271.   "How many teachers would it take to find their way out of a maze?" I am not sure. None have made it out   yet.

272.   "What is the best way to define a mix of emotions?" Seeing your worst enemy drive off a cliff in your   brand-new   car.

273.   "Why does a divorce cost so much?" Because it is worth   every   penny!

274.   "Why is it a good to use valet parking as you get older?" At least they will always remember where the car   is   parked!

275.   "How would a spoiled little rich girl change a light bulb?" She would call up her dad and ask him for a new   apartment.

276.　　"What lettuce was served in the salad bar on the Titanic?"　　　　　　　　　　Iceberg.

277.　　"Why is it that people always walk whenever they play the bagpipes?" Even the people playing the bagpipes want to get away from the terrible music.

278.　　"What happened to the man who lost his left arm, left leg and eye in an accident?" His condition was touch and go, but he is all right now.

279.　　"Why do politicians envy ventriloquists?" Because politicians cannot lie without moving their lips.

280.　　"What do you call a politician who swears to tell the truth?"　　　　A　　　　liar!

281.　　"What is the difference between a fish and a guitar?"　　You　　cannot　　tuna　　fish!

282.　　"Why are there never balloons at Elsa's party?" She　　will　　let　　them　　go!

283.　　"Bay of Bengal is in which state?" Liquid.

284.   "If Mississippi bought Virginia and New Jersey, what would Delaware?" Idaho... Alaska!

285.   "What was the name of the person who made King Arthur's Round Table?" Sir Cumference.

286.   "What do lawyer's wear when they go to court?" Law suits!

287.   "Where do crayons visit when they go on vacation?" Color-ado!

288.   "Why did the belt get arrested?" It was caught holding   up   a   pair   of   pants.

289.   "What do you call a computer that is floating in the ocean?" A Dell rolling down in the Deep!

290.   "What did bacon say to the tomato?" Lettuce get together   soon!

291.   "What do you call a pile of kittens?" A Meow-tain!

292.　"Have you heard about the race between the tomato and the lettuce?" The tomato had to "ketchup" when the lettuce pulled a "head!"

293.　"What do you call a boy who finally stood up to his bullies?" An ambulance!

294.　"What is the name of a computer that can sing a tune?" A – Dell!

295.　"Have you heard about the shampoo shortage in Jamaica?" It is absolutely dread-ful!

296.　"What happens when a cat wins an award at a dog show?" A cat-astrophy!

297.　"What does the femur say to the patella?" I knee-d you!

298.　"What happens when you mix a dark-colored horse with a little cat?" Kitty Perry.

299.　"What do you call an aardvark with three feet?" A yard-vark!

300. "How do you earn a living driving customers away?" Become a driver.

301. "Why is it there so many people with the surname Jones in the telephone book?" Because all of them have telephones!

302. "What do you call a jar of mayonnaise that laughs?" LMAYO.

303. "What is the best way to drown a hipster?" In the mainstream.

304. "What jokes are told in the shower?" Only clean ones!

305. "What do you call coffee that is extremely sad" Despresso!

306. "What happens when a dog swallows a firefly?" He starts to bark with de-light!

307. "What is the one thing that always stays in the corner but is able to travel the world?" A stamp!

308.   "What is the tallest building in the world?" The library because it has the most stories!

309.   "What is the first bet that people make?" The Alpha-bet!

310.   "What happens when you mix a duck with a cow?" You get milk and quakers!

311.   "What did the leopard say after he ate his owner?" Well, that hit the spot!

312.   "What do you call a bull that is taking a nap?" A bull – dozer!

313.   "Why did the computer end up going in to see the doctor?" It had a virus!

314.   "Why are frogs one of the happiest creatures on the planet?" They just eat whatever bugs them!

315.   "What is brown and has a head and tail, but never any legs?" A penny.

316.   "Why did the banana go to the doctors?" It was not   peeling   well.

317.   "What is it called when you have your grandma on   speed   dial"   Insta-gram!

318.   "Why is England the wettest country on Earth?" The queen was reigned there for years and years!

319.   "What do you call a snowman that is a gangster?" Froze- T.

320.   "What is something that you own but others use more   than   you   do?"   Your   name!

321.   "Why do some fish only live in salt water?" The pepper   makes   them   have   to   sneeze!

322.   "Why did the man put all his money into the freezer?" He was hoping to get some cold, hard cash!

323.   "What has just one head and one foot, but has four   legs?"   A   bed!

324.   "What is the biggest difference between a teacher and a locomotive?" A train says, 'chew, chew,

chew,' but the teacher says, 'spit that gum out!'

325.   "Why did the bird have to go see its doctor?" It was   time   for   its   tweet-ment.

326.   "What is the best day of the week to go visit the beach?"   Sun-day   of   course!

327.   "What happens when a frog is parked illegally?" He   gets   toad.

328.   "What is the best season for jumping on the trampoline?"   Spring   time!

329.   "Where does a computer go to dance the night away?"   The   disc   –   o.

330.   "What are the three types of candy that are always in every school?" Smarties, dumdums, and nerds!

331.   "What noises can you hear when two porcupines kiss?"   Ouch!

332.   "Why was one man frisking the other in the restaurant?" His friend said that dinner was on him!

Chapter 3: Potty Humor Can Be The Best Humor

1. "Why was Tigger always so smelly? He was always playing with Pooh!"

2. "The Worst thing about diarrhea is having to spell it!"

3. "Why can you not hear a pterodactyl in the bathroom? The 'P' is silent."

4. "I am a little worried. I swallowed a bunch of scrabble tiles last night. My next poop might spell disaster!"

5. "Why did the letter 'A' go to the bathroom and then come out the letter 'I?' Because he had a vowel movement."

6. "You are American before you go into the bathroom, and an American when you leave, but while you are in there you are European."

7. "Did you hear about the recent scientific find that diarrhea is hereditary? They say it runs in your jeans!"

8. "My friend George and his wife went to the doctor's the other day for their annual physicals. The Doctor asked George how he was doing, emotionally, mentally, and spiritually. George told the doctor his prayers were answered. Every time he went to the bathroom in the night magically the lights turned on and then off when he was done. When his wife heard this she cried, 'George, you are peeing in the fridge again!'"

9. "There is a new wine coming out of Napa Valley these days. It is a combination of Pinot Blanc, Pinot Noir, and Pinot Grigio and is meant to be an anti-diuretic. They are calling it Pinot More! I just heard about it through the   grapevine."

10. "Several little boys were worried about not being baptized so they asked the janitor in their school to do it. He took each of the boys and dunked their heads in the toilet. The boys went out to play and when the other kids asked what religion they were baptized in they said,   'E-piss-copalians!'"

11. "The bathroom doors on the funeral home took your mom and I by surprise. There was a 'His' and a 'Hearse.'"

12. "Your dear Aunt Cora had to go to the doctor the other day. She has some troublesome constipation. The doctor asked is she was doing anything about it, and being her silly old self, she said she sits in the bathroom for at least a half hour morning and night. The doctor of course clarified, and asked if she was taking anything. Your Aunt Cora said, 'Of course! I bring in a magazine!'"

13. "During a job interview four men were asked what was the fastest thing they knew. One replied saying it was a thought popping into his head, another said blinking his eyes, and the third said a light turning on from a switch. When the fourth man answered he said diarrhea. When asked to clarify, he explained that before he could think about it, blink an eye, or turn on the light he had crapped his pants. Obviously the fourth man got the job!"

14. "Two men go into a bathroom. While sitting down, the first man hears the second ask, 'So how are you?' A little bewildered the first man replies, 'good....' The second man then says, 'Where are you going?' And again the first man, still a little nervous, says, 'Alberta.' He waited for another uncomfortable question from the second man when the second man says, 'I am going to

have to call you back. Some weirdo in here thinks I am talking to him!'"

15. "Your mom loves the new house but she did complain to me the other day about the bathroom. She does not like the fact that the neighbors can see her taking a bath. I told her not to worry, if the neighbors do see her in the bath they would buy their own curtains!"

16. "At the local middle school a lot of the girls started wearing lipstick. They would sneak into the bathrooms and put it on. My friend, Joe, is the janitor there and was telling me about how they kept kissing the mirror, leaving little lip marks all over it that he had to clean up. He got fed up and had the principle call all the girls into the bathroom to explain how difficult it was to clean up their mess every night. The principle asked Joe to show the girls how he cleaned the mirror. He took his squeegee and dunked it in a toilet and wiped the mirror clean. He said the girls do not kiss that mirror   any   more!"

17. "At Sunday School your mom was asking the kids where Jesus was. A few replied with things like 'Heaven' and 'in my heart.' I chimed in, 'I know! He is in our bathroom! Every morning when your teacher

gets up she yells, 'Jesus! You are still in here!' She was not amused with my answer."

18. "An Irishman, a Japanese man, and an American were in a sauna. There was a beep, and the American apologized for his phone and turned it off by pressing a button implanted in his arm. Another beep sounded and the Japanese man apologized for his phone and pressed a button in his finger tip. The Irishman was feeling low-tech so he stepped out of the sauna. He came back a little later with toilet paper sticking out of his pants. The other two looked at him funny. He said, 'Sorry! I am getting a fax!'"

19. "Why do you not want to take a Pokemon to the bathroom? It might Pikachu!"

20. "When I went to London I needed to pee pretty bad. I could not find a bathroom so I went to a side street to do my business. A policeman showed up and told me I could not do it where I was at. He told me to follow him and he showed me a private garden on the other side of a fence. He said I could go there. When I asked him if this was just him being a polite British official, he replied, 'No, this is the French Embassy.'"

21. "When does Denzel Washington visit the Rugrats? On Potty Training Day!"

22. "What did the poop say to the fart? You blow me away!"

23. "Why did the toilet paper want to roll down the hill? He needed to get to the bottom!"

24. "What is 20 feet long and smells like urine? A conga line at a nursing home!"

25. "Why could the toilet paper not cross the road? It was stuck in a crack!"

26. "Why did the police officer sit on the toilet? To do his duty!"

27. "Why does the elephant bring his own toilet paper to a party? Because he is a party pooper!"

28. "Why is it impossible to hear a psychiatrist use the bathroom? Because the 'P' is silent."

29. "What is the name of the bathroom superhero? Flush Gordon."

30. "What bathroom do bees like to use? One at a BP station!"

31. "What did the little kid say to the toilet? Did you order a number two? Because I have one ready for you!"

32. "Why do blondes leave their iPhones outside when they go to the bathroom? So they do not give away their IP address."

33. "What can you expect to find in Superman's bathroom? A   Superbowl!"

34. "What is the name of the fairy that lives in the bathroom? Stinker Bell!"

35. "You know what song I sing when I have toe clean up the toilet your mom clogged up? 'Mop in the Name of Love!'"

36. "Why does KFC never have toilet paper? It is finger lickin' good!"

37. "What happens when you mix a Snuggie with a Sham Wow? A heck of a good reason to pee in your pants!"

38. "Why does Chuck Norris have to constantly flush the toilet when he is using it? He keeps scaring the crap out of it!"

39. "Why did they order a lifetime supply of toilet paper to be sent to the garbage heap? Everyone has to take a dump!"

40. "What is the name of the country with all the pissed-off people? Urination!"

41. " What did one toilet say to the other toilet?" You look flushed!"

42. "Your mom got so fat that when she sat on the toilet the other day it started singing, 'A, B, C, D, E, F, G... Get your fat butt off of me!'"

43. "I think I love my toilet the most out of all the things in our house. We have been through a lot of crap together!"

44. "Poop jokes are not my favorite, but they are a solid number two."

45. "I had the worst nightmare last night. I could not wipe my own butt. It was the crappiest dream ever!"

46. "One a scale of one to ten, urinate."

47. "An old Chinese proverb says, 'A man who digs for watch in toilet, bound to have crappy timing.'"

48. "! "Urine. Urine, who? Urine-secure, don't know what for..."

49. "Your mom sent me some sweet texts the other day. She said, "If you are sleeping, send me your dreams. If you are laughing, send me your smile. If you are eating, send me a bite." I replied, "I am on the toilet. Please advise what I can send you." She did not reply."

50. "A young man wanted to propose to his girlfriend so he went to ask her dad for her hand in marriage. He said, 'You cannot even afford her toilet paper.' The young man replied, 'Do not worry, sir. I am not going to marry a girl who is full of crap!'"

51. "This bar down the street had a magical toilet. Every person that sat on it would be serenaded with a different song. Bob tried it out first and when he came

out he said the toilet sang 'Amazing Grace.' Larry tried it next and it sang 'Star Spangled Banner.' Jerry wanted to try it but when he came out he was rather embarrassed. When the others asked him what the toilet sang to him he said, "Do You See What I See?'"

52. "A little boy asked his teacher if he could go to the bathroom. She said he could as long as he recited the alphabet to her. He sang it out, "A, B, C, D, E, F, G, H, I, J, K, L, M, N, O ... Q...' The teacher interrupted and asked, 'Wait, where is 'P?' The little boy replied, 'It is running half way down my leg.'"

53. "I ordered soup the other day. When the server put it down in front of me there was a fly in it. I asked what it was doing in there, and you know what they said? It is pooping!"

54. "I always say laughter is the best medicine ... unless you have diarrhea."

55. "A lady at the bar was acting all flirty with the bartender the other night. She stroked his face and caressed his big beard. She even ran her fingers across his lips while she played in his hair. She asked him to get the manager but the bartender said the manager

was out and if he could take a message. She kind of whispered to him, but it was loud enough for most of the bar to hear, that the ladies room was out of toilet paper, hand soap and paper towels!"

56. "A chief was constipated one day and sent his most trusted warrior to the witch doctor for help. The warrior told the doctor, 'Big chief, no poop.' The doctor gave him a little tablet to give to the chief. The next day, the warrior was back saying, 'Big chief, no poop.' So this time the doctor gave him a handful of the tablets. The warrior came back on the third day and said again, "Big chief, no poop," so the doctor gave him a whole container full of the tablets to give to the chief. The doctor was surprised to see the warrior coming back again on the fourth day, but this time the warrior said to him, 'Big poop! No chief.'"

57. "A little boy saw a man driving a big truck filled with manure. He asked the man what he was going to do with all that poop. The man told the little boy it was to put on his strawberries. The little boy looked concerned for a little bit, and then shrugged. He told the man, 'That is interesting. I do not know where you grew up, but where I come from we put sugar on ours!"

58. "Have you heard about that chronically constipated mathematician? He had to work it out with a pencil!"

59. "What do you call a vegetarian suffering from diarrhea? A salad shooter!"

60. "What is firm and brown? The Brown Family Law Firm!"

61. "My friend Bill got arrested the other night for taking a poo. He said he was sitting there minding his own business when the police came knocking and demanding that he open the door. He explained that he was pooping. The police replied, 'We know sir, the phone booth has glass sides.'"

62. "You know, life starts off with everyone cheering you on when you poop and then it goes down dramatically after that."

63. The kinds of poop according to your dad:

   a. "Ghost" – You feel it come out, you see it on the toilet paper, but you cannot find it in the toilet.

b. "Clean" – You feel it come out, you see it in the toilet, but you do not see it on the toilet paper.

c. "Wet" – You wipe over and over but never feel fresh. You wind up shoving toilet paper into your jeans to keep your undies from getting the skids.

d. "Second Wave" – You just went poop. You wiped and flushed. You are pulling up your pants and realize about half way up that you are not done pooping yet and have to pull your pants down to go   again.

e. "Brain Hemorrhage" – This is also sometimes called the "pop a vein poop." You have to strain so hard to get it to come out that you turn purple and   almost   have   a   stroke!

f. "Lincoln Logs" – This poop is long and strong. You do not want to flush a full log down so you have to grab the plunger and break it apart first.

g. "Notorious Drinker" – This is the poop after a bender. The streak it leaves in the bowl when you   flush   is   the   give   away   trademark.

h. "Gosh, I Wish I Could..." – Your huddled on the toilet, straining and farting, but try as you might, nothing is coming out.

i. "Wet Cheeks" – This is also sometimes called the "power poop." The poop comes out so fast and furious that it splashes your cheeks with toilet water when it hits.

j. "Painted Pottery" – This is also sometimes called the "liquid poop." This poop shoots out of your bum, burning on its way out, and then splashes all around the bowl, coating it in the brown-yellow liquid.

k. "Mexican Food" – This needs know explanation but it is a league of its own.

l. "Crowd Pleaser" – It is an award-winning poop. You need to take a picture or show someone how impressive it is before you flush. The size alone or the appearance can determine if it is a pleaser, or it can be a combination of both.

m. "Mood Enhancer" – After suffering from constipation for an extended period of time, this relief comes just in time, restoring you to your previous awesome self!

n. "Ritual" – Same time, same place, always with the support of a newspaper.

o. "Guinness Book of Records" – It is so impressive you do not just want to show it off, like a "Crowd Pleaser," but want to also preserve its memory for future generations.

p. "Aftershock" – This poop leaves a stink bomb that lingers for at least seven hours. Anyone that comes in contact with the infected bathroom or about ten feet from it will feel the after effects for the rest of the day.

q. "Honeymoon's Over" – Taking a poop in front of someone else. Enough said.

r. "Groaner" – Vocal support is needed to help get out this huge poop.

s. "Floater" – Not only is it buoyant right after, but it has a way of finding its way to the surface again   even   after   being   flushed.

t. "Ranger" – This is also sometimes called the "Stage 5 Clinger." This poop refuses to let go of the butt. You can bounce or rock to try to get it to detach but most likely you will have to push or pull it away with the assistance of a bit of toilet paper.

u. "Phantom" – No one it taking credit for a poop left in the toilet. Its history is a mystery.

v. "Peek-a-poo" – This poop peeks its head out but goes back in. You need serious muscle control and a lot of patience to coax it out.

w. "Bombshell" – This unsuspected poo sneaks up on you at the worst times, like during a dentist appointment or while making love, or when you are   nowhere   near   a   bathroom.

x. "Snake Charmer" – This skinny poo magically curls itself up in the bowl, looking a little ominous, but do not worry, it is usually harmless.

y. "Olympic" – Precisely one hour before any sporting event this poo appears. It look's strikingly similar to "Notorious Drinker" poop.

z. "Back to Nature" – This poop can really be any type of poo, but you have to deposit it in the woods or behind an open passenger side door.

aa. "Divine Pebbles" – These little clusters of poop balls are a relief when you finally see them collected in the bowl.

bb. "Premeditated" – You used a laxative. This does not count. Cheater.

cc. "Poozopherenia" – This is deadly. It is a fear of pooping. Seek immediate medical attention.

dd. "Energizer" – This is also sometimes called "Keep on Going." Just never wants to stop. It is best to have a magazine nearby for this one.

ee. "Nuclear" – Possibly the worst poop you can have. This is like having the "Bombshell" and "Second Wave" at the same time. There is an element of "Aftershock" present as well. It feels like it is ripping you a new one and hurts like hell. Typically happens when you eat a ghost pepper.

ff. "Power Dump" – You can barely get your pants down by the time this one comes out.

gg. "Liquid Plumper" – You should have paid attention to the "Lincoln Log." This poop was so big it clogged your toilet. Now it is overflowing onto your floor.

hh. "Spinal Tap" – This one hurts so bad it feels like the log is inching its way out sideways.

ii. "I'm Giving Birth Through My Butt" – This is very similar to the "Lincoln Log" and the "Spinal Tap." It is large and thick, and hurts like hell. The main difference is the cavernous air pocket it leaves in your rectum afterwards.

jj. "Porridge" – This poop is like toothpaste and keeps squeezing out of you. You need to decide to flush every now and then otherwise it will pile up in the toilet bowl and you risk it reaching up to your butt cheeks.

kk. "I Better Chew Better Next Time" – This is especially noticeable after consuming a bag of Doritos too quickly. When the little shards are coming out it is like a Calvary of razor blades slicing you up on the inside until they splash into the bowl.

ll. "Bunny Turds" – These cute little marble-like droppings hits water with a little splash.

mm. "What In The Hell Died?!" – This is also sometimes called the "Toxic Turd." The best part of this dump is waiting nearby, not warning anyone, and watching them run in horror after they gag on the stench.

nn. "I Know You Are Still Hanging There" – This clinger is holding on for dear life and will not drop off. You just sit there waiting because you know if you wipe now it will just end up smearing all over you cheeks.

oo. "There is Poo on Your Shoe, You Poo-shoe Bastard!" – You know the culprit. No need to explain further.

64. "Your mom went to the doctor and they handed her one of those urine cups. The nurse told her to go into the bathroom and that the doctor would be with her shortly. A few minutes later your mom walked out, with a relieved look, and said, 'Thanks, but I do not need this cup. There was a working toilet in there after all!'"

65. "A man walks into a bar. The bartender asks him what he wants and the man orders a Bud Light. The bartender brought him his drink and noticed he was talking into his hand like a phone. When the bartender asked him what he was doing he explained that he was struck by lightening and now his hand worked like a cellphone. Of course he did not believe him, but the man dialed the number of the bar on his hand and the phone rang. Later in the evening the man went into the restroom and did not come out for several minutes. Worried, the bartender went in to see if he was ok. When he walked in the man was standing there with his pants down and toilet paper hanging out from his butt. When the bartender asked what was going on, the man replied, 'I will be out in a minute. I am getting a fax!'"

66. "We dropped your grandmother off at the nursing home the other day. She seemed to be well cared for. They helped her bathe, fed her delicious meals, and

even found her a lovely spot in a rocking chair near the window that looks out over the lake. The nurses did mention that she had a tendency to lean over to one side, but they always were right there to help her sit straight again. Apparently it happened over and over again. When we asked your grandma how she liked her new home, she said, 'It is alright. The only problem is that they never let you fart!'"

67. "Two old folks climbed into bed. The man lets out a fart and says, 'seven points!' The woman asks him what that was all about and he replies, 'I am playing fart football!' A few minutes later the woman lets out a fart and says, 'touchdown! Tie game.' It takes a few minutes for the man to take the lead with another fart but the woman follows not very long after. This goes on for a few more minutes, with the woman taking the lead with a little field goal squeaker. The man was determined not to be beaten by his wife, so he pushes really hard. He gives it all he has and ends up pooping in the bed. The woman asks, 'What was that?' and the man replies, 'half time. Time to switch sides!'"

68. "Back in the day there were men called the 'town fathers.' Their role was to find ways to motivate the towns people to participate more during the regular

town meetings. One of the ideas was to bring in a hypnotist. Willing to try just about anything, they brought one in who was famous in the area. It was publicized all over town that this hypnotist was coming and everyone was excited. The plan worked and the next town meeting was packed with all the people coming to see the hypnotist. The hypnotists stood up and withdrew a pocket watch from his pocket. He began swinging it back and forth telling the towns people, 'Watch the watch... watch the watch ....'' As the watch swung back and forth the people became mesmerized. Everyone was watching the shiny watch swing back and forth. Suddenly, the hypnotist accidently dropped the watch and it fell with a crack on the floor. The hypnotist cried, 'Crap!' It took the town father's over three weeks to clean up the town hall."

69. "What is invisible to the naked eye but can be easily noticed when it is broken? Wind!"

70. "A small family of moles lived in a little hole near the local breakfast restaurant. One day the mother mole popped up out of the hole and sniffed the air. She explained, 'I smell pancakes! Yum!' The father mole was excited to smell what was for breakfast so he popped his head up and exclaimed, 'Oh! That smells

like hash browns! Delicious!' Curious about what he could smell, the little baby mole tried to stick his head out and smell the air, but his way was blocked by his mother and father. He piped up, 'Oh man, all I smell is molasses.'"

71. "A couple of old men were eating next to me at the restaurant the other day. One man started looking at the other one kind of funny and said, 'Hey Joe, There is something funny about your ear. Is that a suppository you have stuffed in there?' It took the other man to finally get Joe to understand what he was saying, but finally Joe pulled the thing out of his ear. Turns out it was a suppository. After awhile, Joe said to the other man, 'Thank God you saw this thing! I think I know where my other hearing aid is now.'"

72. "A minivan loaded down with all sorts of supplies crept into the only open campsite. Four kids scrambled out of the van and began unloading gear frantically. Then they started setting up the tent. In the frenzy, the boys took off to gather the firewood and the girls began to help set up the camp stove and put out the utensils for cooking. I was astonished at the team effort and hard work the kids were demonstrating and commended the father for such amazing kids. He gave me a sly smile and

explained, 'I have a system for camping. No one gets to use the restroom until the camp is completely set up.'

73. "Your sister gave me a quiz the other day. She thought it said, 'What kind of father are you?' but what it really said was, 'What kind of farter are you?' The options were:

    a. Sensitive- You cry after you fart.

    b. Miserable- You want to let one out but are incapable of letting it go.

    c. Athletic- Any type of exertion releases a fart.

    d. Intellectual- You have the amazing ability to distinguish what food the person ate that produced the fart.

    e. Sadistic- You like to fart in bed, under the covers, and then quickly pull them up over the head of your bed partner.

    f. Strategic- You fart but try to cover the sound of it with a loud cough.

g. Anti-social- You do not fart in public. Whenever the need arises you sneak off to another room to let it go in private.

h. Thrifty- You never know when you need a good fart so you always keep a few in stock.

i. Foolish- You hold in your farts for hours or even days   at   a   time!

j. Dishonest- Every time you fart you blame someone or something else, including the baby and   the   dog.

k. Honest- You publicly admit to your farting, but offer up a medical reason for having to have done   so.

l. Nervous- You start farting, but then stop half way   through.

m. Scientific- You are a consistent farter, but are concerned about its effects on global warming and the levels of pollution in your area.

n. Unfortunate- You feel a fart coming on and attempt to let it go, but end up pooping your pants   instead.

o. Impudent- You have no shame. You fart as loud as you can make it and then laugh even louder!

p. Shy- You hold back your farts, trying to make them as quiet as possible, and blush constantly while it is happening and even after.

q. Proud- You are not ashamed of your farts. In fact, you actually think they are pretty fantastic.

r. Amiable- You love the smell of your farts, but you also love the smell of other people's farts, too!

s. Vain- You only love to smell the special aroma of your own farts and no one else's."

74. "There is a magical scale in the airport in Atlanta. Your mother told me this amazing story about her encounter with it one time. She was flying on her way to Boston, when she decided to give the scale a try. It showed on the screen the following message, 'You are 135 pounds

and are travelling to Boston.' She sat down a little surprised but thought she should probably try it again to see if it tells her the same thing. This time the message said, 'You are 135 pounds, are travelling to Boston, and you are going to play the fiddle.' Your mom laughed out loud. You know she does not play an instrument. But when she sat back down in her seat a man placed a case with a fiddle next to her and asked if she wanted to play. She decided to give it a shot and the music was amazing. Wanting to find out what the scale would say next she stepped up onto it again. This time is said, 'You are 135 pounds, are travelling to Boston, have played a fiddle, and will pass gas soon.' Your mom was always a shy farter and had never tooted in public before. But as she went to get off the scale, she tripped over and passed gas when she fell over.' Startled at what was happening, she jumped up and stood on the scale again. This time, the screen displayed, 'You are 135 pounds, you have fiddled and farted around today, and just missed your flight to Boston!'"

Chapter 4: "Knock, Knock ... Who's There?"

1. Knock knock!

Who is there?

"Cash."

"Cash, who?"

"No thanks, but I will take a peanut if you have one!"

2. Knock knock!

Who is there?

"Banana."

"Banana, who?"

"Banana split!"

3. Knock knock!

Who is there?

"Beets."

"Beets, who?"

"Beets Me!"

4. Knock knock!

Who is there?

"Police."

"Police, who?"

"Police, may I come in? I am asking very politely!"

5. Knock knock!
Who is there?
 "Banana."
"Banana, who?"
"Knock, Knock."
"Who's there?"
"Orange."
"Orange, who?"
"Orange you glad I did not say 'Banana?'"

6. Knock knock!
Who is there?
"Cargo."
"Cargo, who?"
"Cargo beep, beep!"

7. Knock knock!
Who is there?

"Haiti."
"Haiti, who?"
"I Haiti see you go, but it is time to clear out of here."

8. Knock knock!
Who is there?

"Obi Wan."

"Obi Wan, who?"

"You are the Obi Wan for me."

9. Knock knock!

Who is there?

"Kiwi."

"Kiwi, who?"

"Kiwi go to the store?"

10. Knock knock!

Who is there?

"Lettuce."

"Lettuce, who?"

"Lettuce in, we're freezing!"

11. Knock knock!

Who is there?

"Olive."

"Olive, who?"

"Olive right next door to you."

12. Knock knock!

Who is there?

"Turnip."

"Turnip, who?"

"Turnip the volume, it is too quiet in here."

13. Knock knock!

Who is there?

"Police."

"Police, who?"

"Police hurry—I am freezing out here!"

14. Knock knock!

Who is there?

"Doctor."

"Doctor who?"

"You watch that TV show?"

15. Knock knock!

Who is there?

"Orange."

"Orange, who?"

"Orange you glad to see me?"

16. Knock knock!

Who is there?

"India."

"India, who?"

"India afternoon I need a snack."

17. Knock knock!

Who is there?

"Howl."

"Howl, who?"

"Howl you know it is really me unless you open the door?"

18. Knock knock!

Who is there?

"Ada."

"Ada, who?"

"I Ada burger for lunch!"

19. Knock knock!

Who is there?

"Atch."

"Atch, who?"

"Bless you!"

20. Knock knock!

Who is there?

"Wooden shoe."

"Wooden shoe, who?"

"Wooden shoe like to hear another joke?"

21. Knock knock!

Who is there?

"Amy."

"Amy, who?"

"Amy-fraid I have forgotten already!"

22. Knock knock!

Who is there?

"Norma Lee."

"Norma Lee, who?"

"Norma Lee I bring my key with me but I forgot today. That is why I am knocking!"

23. Knock knock!

Who is there?

"Annie."

"Annie, who?"

"Annie body going to open the door already?"

24. Knock knock!

Who is there?

"Needle."

"Needle, who?"

"Needle little help getting in the door."

25. Knock knock!

Who is there?

"Ben."

"Ben, who?"

"I Ben knocking for 20 minutes!"

26. Knock knock!

Who is there?

"Grub."

"Grub, who?"

"Grub a dub, dub. Three men in a tub."

27. Knock knock!

Who is there?

"Doris."

"Doris, who?"

"Doris locked. Open up!"

28. Knock knock!

Who is there?

"Frank."

"Frank, who?"

"Frank you for being my friend!"

29. Knock knock!

Who is there?

"Howard."

"Howard, who?"

"Howard I know?"

30. Knock knock!
Who is there?
"Isabel."
"Isabel, who?"
"Isabel working? I had to knock."

31. Knock knock!
Who is there?
"Justin."
"Justin who?"
"Justin the neighborhood and thought I would come over."

32. Knock knock!
Who is there?
"Ken."
"Ken, who?"
"Ken I come in, it is freezing out here?"

33. Knock knock!
Who is there?
"Kent."
"Kent, who?"
"Kent you tell who I am by my voice?"

34. Knock knock!

Who   is   there?

"Lena."

"Lena, who?"

"Lena little closer and I'll tell you!"

35. Knock knock!

Who is there?

"Luke."

"Luke, who?"

"Luke through the keyhole to see!"

36. Knock knock!

Who   is   there?

"Will   you   remember   me   in   two   minutes?"

"Yes."

"Knock, Knock."

"Who's there?"

"Hey, you did not remember me!"

37. Knock knock!

Who is there?

"Nana."

"Nana, who?"

"Nana your business who is there."

38. Knock knock!

Who is there?

"Nobel."

"Nobel, who?"

"Nobel, that is why I knocked!"

39. Knock knock!

Who is there?

"Otto."

"Otto, who?"

"Otto know what is taking you so long!"

40. Knock knock!

Who is there?

"Sherlock."

"Sherlock, who?" —

"Sherlock your door at night."

41. Knock knock!

Who is there?

"Tyrone."

"Tyrone, who?"

"Tyrone shoelaces!"

42. Knock knock!

Who is there?

"Wendy."

"Wendy, who?"

"Wendy bell works again I will not have to knock anymore."

43. Knock knock!

Who is there?

"Will."

"Will, who?"

"Will you let me in? It is freezing out here!"

44. Knock knock!

Who is there?

"Alpaca."

"Alpaca who?"

"Alpaca the trunk, you pack the suitcase!"

45. Knock knock!

Who is there?

"Cow-go."

"Cow-go, who?"

"No, Cow-go MOO!"

46. Knock knock!

Who is there?

"Goat."

"Goat, who?"

"Goat to the door and find out."

47. Knock knock!

Who is there?

"Honey bee."

"Honey bee, who?"

"Honey bee a dear and get me some juice."

48. Knock knock!

Who is there?

"Monkey."

"Monkey, who?"

"Monkey see. Monkey do."

49. Knock knock!

Who is there?

"Some bunny."

"Some bunny, who?"

"Some bunny has been eating all my carrots!"

50. Knock knock!

Who is there?

"Who."

"Who, who?"

"Is there an owl in here?"

51. Knock knock!

Who is there?

"Yukon."

"Yukon, who?"

"Yukon say that again!"

52. Knock knock!

Who is there?

"Amarillo."

"Amarillo, who?"

"Amarillo nice guy!"

53. Knock knock!

Who is there?

"Amish."

"Amish, who?"

"Amish you, too!"

54. Knock knock!

Who is there?

"Alex."

"Alex who?"

"Hey, Alex the questions around here!"

55. Knock knock!

Who is there?

"Avenue."

"Avenue, who?"

"Avenue knocked on this door before?"

56. Knock knock!

Who is there?

"India."

"India, who?"

"India-ana Jones."

57. Knock knock!

Who is there?

"To."

"To, who?"

"No, it is 'to, whom.'"

58. Knock knock!

Who is there?

"Eva."

"Eva, who?"

"Eva see a chicken cross the road?"

59. Knock knock!

Who is there?

"Beef."

"Beef, who?"

"Beef-ore I get cold, you had better let me in!"

60. Knock knock!

Who is there?

"Aaron."

"Aaron, who?"

"Always Aaron the side of caution when you are walking alone at night."

61. Knock knock!

Who is there?

"Orange."

"Orange, who?"

"Orange you going to answer the door?"

62. Knock knock!

Who is there?

"Someone who cannot get to the bell!"

63. Knock knock!

Who is there?

"Dozen."

"Dozen who?"

"Dozen anyone want to let me in?"

64. Knock knock!

Who is there?

"Lemme"

"Lemme, who?"

"Lemme see inside!"

65. Knock knock!

Who is there?

"Abe."

"Abe, who?"

"Abe C D E F G H..."

66. Knock knock!

Who is there?

"Claire."

"Claire, who?"

"Claire out of the way, I am coming through!"

67. Knock knock!

Who is there?

"Barbie."

"Barbie, who?"

"Barbie Q. Chicken!"

68. Knock knock!

Who is there?

"Weevil."

"Weevil, who?"
"Weevil weevil, rock you!"

69. Knock knock!
Who is there?
"A little old lady."
"A little old lady, who?"
"I did not know you could yodel."

70. Knock knock!
Who is there?
"Broccoli."
"Broccoli, who?"
"Broccoli does not have a last name, silly!"

71. Knock knock!
Who is there?
"Howie."
"Howie, who?"
"Howie going to hide this dead body out here?"

72. Knock knock!
Who is there?
"Ice cream."
"Ice cream, who?"

"Ice cream if you do not let me in!"

73. Knock knock!

Who is there?

"Control freak."

"Cont..."

"Okay, now you say, 'Control freak, who?'"

74. Knock knock!

Who is there?

"Mikey."

"Mikey, who?"

"Mikey doesn't fit in the keyhole!"

75. Knock knock!

Who is there?

"Knock, Knock."

"Who's there?"

"The door is open. Just come in!"

76. Knock knock!

Who is there?

"Water."

"Water, who?"

"Water you doing in my house?"

77.
"I am."
"I am, who?"
"Do you mean you do not know who you are?"

78.
"Alma."
"Alma, who?"
"Alma not going to tell you!"

79. Knock knock!
Who is there?
"Iva."
"Iva, who?"
"Let me in! Iva sore hand from all this knocking!"

80. Knock knock!
Who is there?
"Spell."
"Spell, who?"
"W-h-o."

81. Knock knock!
Who is there?

"Abby."

"Abby, who?"

"Abby birthday to you!"

82. Knock knock!

Who is there?

"Roach."

"Roach, who?"

"I Roach you an email, did you get it?"

83. Knock knock!

Who is there?

"I eat map."

"I eat map, who?"

"Gross!"

84. Knock knock!

Who is there?

"King Tut."

"King Tut, who?"

"I brought King Tut-key fried chicken!"

85. Knock knock!

Who is there?

"Broken pencil."

"Broken pencil, who?"

"Never mind this joke, it is pointless."

86. Knock knock!

Who is there?

"Witches."

"Witches, who?"

"Witches the way home?"

87. Knock knock!

Who is there?

"Me."

"Me, who?"

"Wow, they were not kidding you lost it when you got hit in your head."

88. Knock knock!

Who is there?

"Mary and Abbey."

"Mary and Abbey, who?"

"Marry Christmas and Abbey New Year!"

89. Knock knock!

Who is there?

"I did up."

"I did up, who?"

"Hope you flushed the toilet!"

90. Knock knock!

Who is there?

"Interrupting cow."

"Interrupt...."

"Moo!"

91. Knock knock!

Who is there?

"Shelby."

"Shelby, who?"

"Shelby coming round the mountain when she comes."

92. Knock knock!

Who is there?

"Woo."

"Woo, who?"

"It is just a joke, you do not need to get so excited."

93. Knock knock!

Who is there?

"Gray Z."

"Gray Z., who?"

"You are one Gray Z. mixed up kid."

94. Knock knock!

Who is there?

"Annie."

"Annie, who?"

"Annie thing you can do, I can do better."

95. Knock knock!

Who is there?

"Amos."

"Amos, who?"

"Amos-quito bit me and it itches!"

96. Knock knock!

Who is there?

"Wire."

"Wire, who?"

"Wire are you always asking me who is there?"

97. Knock knock!

Who is there?

"Witch"

"Witch, who?"

Witch one of you will give me the time?"

98. Knock knock!

Who is there?

"Robin."

"Robin, who?"

"I am Robin you. Hand over your wallet."

99. Knock knock!

Who is there?

"Howl."

"Howl, who?"

"Howl do you know if you never open this door?"

100. Knock knock!

Who is there?

"Owl says."

"Owl says, who?"

"Yes, they do say, 'Who!'"

101. Knock knock!

Who is there?

"Art."

"Art, who?"

"Art-oo D2, of course!"

102. Knock knock!

Who is there?

"Kanga."

"Kanga, who?"

"It is actually kanga-roo."

103. Knock knock!

Who is there?

"Deja."

"Deja, who?"

"Knock, Knock!"

104. Knock knock!

Who is there?

"No one."

"No one, who?"

*Do not say anything!"

105. Knock knock!

Who is there?

"Extraterrestrial."

"Extraterrestrial, who?"

"Honestly, how many extraterrestrials do you know?"

106. Knock knock!

Who is there?

"Opportunity."

"Opportunity, who?"

"Do not ask, just open! Opportunity never knocks twice!"

107. Knock knock!

Who is there?

"Says."

"Says, who?"

"Says me, that is who."

108. Knock knock!

Who is there?

"Stopwatch."

"Stopwatch, who?"

"Stopwatch you are doing and pay attention."

109. Knock knock!

Who is there?

"Europe."

"Europe, who?"

"No, I am not! Europe-oo!"

110. Knock knock!

Who is there?

"Candice."

"Candice, who?"

"Candice door open, or no?"

111. Knock knock!

Who is there?

"Needle."

"Needle, who?"

"I needle money for the movies tonight."

112. Knock knock!

Who is there?

"Two knee."

"Two knee, who?"

"Two knee fish."

113. Knock knock!

Who is there?

"Closure."

"Closure, who?"

"Closure mouth when you are chewing!"

114. Knock knock!

Who is there?

"Godiva."

"Godiva, who?"

"Godiva terrible headache today. Do you have an aspirin?"

115. Knock knock!

Who is there?

"Loaf."

"Loaf, who?"

"I do not just like bread, I loaf it!"

116. Knock knock!

Who is there?

"Pecan."

"Pecan, who?"

"Pecan someone your own size for a change."

117. Knock knock!

Who is there?

"Scold."

"Scold, who?"

"Scold outside—let me in!"

118. Knock knock!

Who is there?

"Wanda."

"Wanda, who?"

"Wanda hang out here or at my place?"

119. Knock knock!

Who is there?

"Ho ho."

"Ho ho, who?"

"I do not think you are going to get that gig as Santa. Your impression needs a little work."

120. Knock knock!

Who   is   there?

"Hanna."

"Hanna,   who."

"Hanna partridge in a pear tree!"

121. Knock knock!

Who is there?

"Xavier."

"Xavier, who?"

"Xavier breath and open the door!"

122. Knock knock!

Who is there?

"Irish."

"Irish, who?"

"Irish you a Merry Christmas."

123. Knock knock!

Who is there?

"Dwight."

"Dwight, who?"

"Dwight way is always better than the wrong way!"

124. Knock knock!

Who is there?

"Convex."

"Convex, who?"

"Convex go to prison."

125. Knock knock!

Who is there?

"Ya."

"Ya, who?"

"Awww, I am excited to see you, too!"

126. Knock knock!

Who is there? "Ice cream." "Ice cream, who?"
"ICE CREAM UNTIL YOU OPEN THIS DOOR!"

127. Knock knock!

Who is there?

"Somebody."

"Somebody, who?"

"Somebody who cannot reach your doorbell!"

128. Knock knock!

Who is there?

"Nun."

"Nun, who?"

"Nun of your business!"

129. Knock knock!

Who is there?

"I smell mop."

"I smell mop, who?"

"Ewww, that is gross!"

130. Knock knock!

Who is there?

"I eat mop."

"I eat mop, who?"

"That is even worse than smelling it!"

131. Knock knock!

Who is there?

"Dewey."

"Dewey, who?"

"Dewey have to go out tonight?"

132. Knock knock!

Who is there?

"Razor hands."

"Razor hands, who?"

"Razor hands, this is a stick up!"

133. Knock knock!

Who is there?

"Alec."

"Alec, who?"

"Alec-tricity is shocking, is it not?"

134. Knock knock!

Who is there?

"Stupid."

"Stupid, who?"

"Stupid you, that is who!"

135. Knock knock!

Who is there?

"Thermos."

"Thermos, who?"

"Thermos be a better way to get in than always knocking!"

136. Knock knock!

Who is there?

"Water."

"Water, who?"

"Water you doing? Just open the door already!"

137. Knock knock!

Who is there?

"Euripides."

"Euripides, who?"

"If Euripides jeans you will have to pay for them!"

138. Knock knock!

Who is there?

"Tank."

"Tank, who?

"You are welcome!"

139. Knock knock!

Who is there?

"Oswald."

"Oswald, who?"

"Oswald my gum again. Darn!"

140. Knock knock!

Who is there?

"Butter."

"Butter, who?"

"Butter nut tell your mom about this!"

141. Knock knock!

Who is there?

"Snow."

"Snow, who?"

"It Snow use, I have forgotten my name again...."

142. Knock knock!

Who is there?

"Anita."

"Anita, who?"

"Anita to borrow a pen!"

143. Knock knock!

Who is there?

"Ren."

"Ren, who?"

"Ren is dinner? I am so hungry!"

144. Knock knock!

Who is there?

"Yacht."

"Yacht, who?"

"Yacht-a know me by now. Let me in!"

145. Knock knock!

Who is there?

"Iguana."

"Iguana, who?"

"Iguana hold your hand."

146. Knock knock!

Who is there?

"Haden."

"Haden, who?"

"Want to play Haden go seek with me?"

147. Knock knock!

Who is there?

"I love."

"I love, who?"

"Well, how am I supposed to know who you love? You tell me!"

148. Knock knock!

Who is there?

"Zeke."

"Zeke, who?"

"Can we play hide and go Zeke now?"

149. Knock knock!

Who is there?

"Cantaloupe."

"Cantaloupe, who?"

"I cantaloupe. I am married to your mom!"

150. Knock knock!

Who   is   there?

"Chicken."

"Chicken, who?"

"Why not chicken your pockets for my key so I do not have to knock anymore!"

151. Knock knock!

Who is there?

"Juicy."

"Juicy, who?"

"Juicy what I just saw?"

152. Knock knock!

Who is there?

"Candice."

"Candice, who?"

"Candice night of jokes from your old man get any better?"

153. Knock knock!

Who is there?

"Snow."

"Snow, who?"

"There is snow business like show business!"

154. Knock knock!

Who is there?

"Urine."

"Urine, who?"

"Urine in serious trouble if you do not open this door for me!"

155. Knock knock!

Who is there?

"Ben."

"Ben, who?"

"Ben Down and Lick My Boots."

156. Knock knock!

Who is there?

"Radio."

"Radio, who?"

"Radio not, here I come!

157. Knock knock!

Who is there?

"From."

"From, who?"

"Actually, grammatically speaking, you should say 'From whom.'"

158. Knock knock!

Who is there?

"Ivana."

"Ivana, who?"

"Open up, Ivana come in!"

159. Knock knock!

Who is there?

"Juno."

"Juno, who?"

"Juno I love you, right?"

160. Knock knock!

Who   is   there?

"Value."

"Value, who?"

"Value you please come over here so I can give you a hug?"

161. Knock knock!

Who is there?

"Disguise."

"Disguise, who?"

"Do not be embarrassed disguise your dad!"

162. Knock knock!

Who is there?

"Kook."

"Kook, who?"

"Hey! Do not call me cookoo!"

163. Knock knock!

Who is there?

"Dishes."

"Dishes, who?"

"Dishes me, who are you?"

164. Knock knock!

Who is there?

"Frank."

"Frank, who?"

"Frank you for letting me be your dad!"

165. Knock knock!

Who is there?

"Daisy."

"Daisy, who?"

"Daisy me rollin', they hatin'!"

166. Knock knock!

Who is there?

"Pencil."

"Pencil, who?"

"Your pencil fall down if you do not wear a belt, son."

167. Knock knock!

Who is there?

"Aardvark."

"Aardvark, who?"

"Aardvark 5,000 miles... just to be the man that'd walk 5,000 miles to stand outside your door."

168. Knock knock!

Who is there?

"The guy who finished second."

"The guy who finished second, who?"

"Exactly."

169. Knock knock!

Who is there?

"Tunis."

"Tunis, who?"

"Tunis company, three is a crowd!"

170. Knock knock!

Who is there?

"Dwayne."

"Dwayne, who?"

"Hurry! Dwayne the tub, it is overflowing!"

171. Knock knock!

Who is there?

"Iran."

"Iran, who?"

"Iran over to tell you this joke!"

172. Knock knock!

Who is there?

"Leaf."

"Leaf, who?"

"Leaf Me Alone!"

173. Knock knock!

Who is there?

Dad: Hey! I know this awesome joke.

You: Tell me!

Dad: Sure. You start with, "."

You: Ok. "."

Dad: ""

174. Knock knock!

Who is there?

"Cereal."

"Cereal, who?"

"Cereal nice to meet you!"

175. Knock knock!

Who is there?

"Nuisance.""Nuisance, who?"

"What is nuisance yesterday?"

176. Knock knock!

Who is there?

"Hippa."

"Hippa, who?"

"I am so sorry but I cannot disclose that information to you."

177. Knock knock!

Who is there?

"Yourself."

"Yourself, who?"

"Yourself – one is ringing. Are you going to answer it?"

178. Knock knock!

Who is there?

"Eileen."

"Eileen, who?"

"I am so sorry. Eileen'd on the door and it broke!"

179. Knock knock!

Who is there?

"Snow."

"Snow, who?"

"A snow man named Frosty!"

180. Knock knock!

Who is there?

"Denial."

"Denial, who?"

"Denial is in Egypt, silly!"

181. Knock knock!

Who is there?

"Snow."

"Snow, who?"

"Snow boots allowed in the house? I can take them off!"

182. Knock knock!

Who is there?

"Snow."

"Snow, who?"

"Snow use, I do not remember my name."

183. Knock knock!

Who is there?

"Snow."

"Snow, who?"

"Snow more presents will be under the trees if you do not open up!"

184. Knock knock!

Who is there?

"Snow."

"Snow, who?"

"It is a snow day! Go back to sleep!"

185. Knock knock!

Who is there?

"Al."

"Al, who?"

"Al give you a kit kat for your snicker's!"

186. Knock knock!

Who is there?

"Dishes."

"Dishes who?"

"Dishes a nice place you got here."

187. Knock knock!

Who is there?

"Aida."

"Aida, who?"

"I Aida a whole carton of ice cream and am not feeling very well."

188. Knock knock!

Who is there?

"Armageddon."

"Armageddon, who?"

"Armageddon outta here and so should you!"

189. Knock knock!

Who is there?

"Fangs."

"Fangs, who?"

"Fangs for finally letting me in!"

190. Knock knock!

Who is there?

"Frank."

"Frank, who?"

"Frankenstein, arrrrrgggghhhh...."

191. Knock knock!

Who is there?

"Hardy."

"Hardy, who?"

"I hardy recognize you. Have you been working out?"

192. Knock knock!

Who is there?

"Harry."

"Harry, who?"

"I am a Harry monster coming after you! Run!"

193. Knock knock!

Who is there?

"Hugo."

"Hugo, who?"

"Hugo put on your coat and we can go to the movies together."

194. Knock knock!

Who is there?

"Boo."

"Boo, who?"

"I want some Boo berry ice cream. Do you?"

195. Knock knock!

Who is there?

"Butcher."

"Butcher, who?"

"Butcher stuff in my pockets so you do not have to bring your bag."

196. Knock knock!

Who is there?

"Candy."

"Candy, who?"

"Candy boys come over for poker tonight?"

197. Knock knock!

Who is there?

"Chuck."

"Chuck, who?"

"Chuck and see that you turned off the iron before you leave the house."

198. Knock knock!

Who is there?

"Celeste."

"Celeste, who?"

"When was Celeste time you opened the door for anyone?"

199. Knock knock!

Who is there?

"Curry"

"Curry, who?"

"Can you Curry my keys, please?"

200. Knock knock!

Who is there?

"Datsum."

"Datsum, who?"

"Datsum nice landscaping you have out here!"

201. Knock knock!

Who is there?

"Canoe."

"Canoe, who?"

"Canoe come out and play with me today?"

202. Knock knock!

Who is there?

"Falafel."

"Falafel, who?"

"I Falafel after eating all that crap."

203. Knock knock!

Who is there?

"Fozzle."

"Fozzle, who?"

"Fozzle last time, let me in!"

204. Knock knock!

Who is there?

"Adelia."

"Adelia, who?"

"Adelia the cards and then we can play poker!"

205. Knock knock!

Who is there?

"Adolph."

"Adolph, who?"

"Adolph ball hit me in my mouff. That dis why I am talking dis way."

206. Knock knock!

Who is there?

"Andy."

"Andy, who?"

"Andy winner is ...."

207. Knock knock!

Who is there?

"Beecher."

"Beecher, who?"

"I will Beecher at any game you choose."

208. Knock knock!

Who is there?

"Meow."

"Meow, who?"

"Take meow to the ball game, take me out with the crowd!"

209. Knock knock!

Who is there?

"Harvey."

"Harvey, who?"

"Harvey going to play this game forever or will you finally accept defeat?"

210. Knock knock!

Who is there?

"James."

"James, who?"

"Oh, the James we play!"

211. Knock knock!

Who is there?

"Les."

"Les, who?"

"Les go play a round of golf today!"

212. Knock knock!

Who is there?

"Omega."

"Omega, who?"

"Omega best man win!"

213. Knock knock!

Who is there?

"Raoul."

"Raoul, who?"

"You need to Raoul with the punches!"

214. Knock knock!

Who is there?

"Scold."

"Scold, who?"

"It scold enough to go ice skating finally!"

215. Knock knock!

Who is there?

"Soccer."

"Soccer, who?"

"Your soccer in the drawer like always."

216. Knock knock!

Who is there?

"Tahiti."

"Tahiti, who?"

"Tahiti homerun you need to practice with a great coach."

217. Knock knock!

Who is there?

"Tennis."

"Tennis, who?"

"Tennis adding five plus five."

218. Knock knock!

Who is there?

"Tennis."

"Tennis, who?"

"Tennis – see!"

219. Knock knock!

Who is there?

"Tennyson."

"Tennyson, who?"

"Tennys - son, is a great game!"

220. Knock knock!

Who is there?

"Uriah."

"Uriah, who?"

"Keep Uriah on the ball so you do not miss it!"

221. Knock knock!

Who is there?

"Wanda."

"Wanda, who?"

"Wanda play a game with me?"

222. Knock knock!

Who is there?

"Eeyore."

"Eeyore, who?"

"Eeyore not to 'E.' That is the question."

223. Knock knock!

Who is there?

"Eeyore."

"Eeyore, who?"

"Eeyore is locked, please let me in now!"

224. Knock knock!

Who is there?

Gopher.

"Gopher, who?"

"Gopher the gold, son!"

225. Knock knock!

Who is there?

<u>Gopher.</u>

"Gopher, who?"

"Gopher's like to goph at the goph course."

226. Knock knock!

Who is there?

"Piglet."

"Piglet, who?"

"Pig, let me in! It is too cold out here."

227. Knock knock!

Who is there?

"Pooh."

"Pooh, who?"

"Awwww, you do not need to cry!"

228. Knock knock!

Who is there?

"Rabbit."

"Rabbit, who?"

"Rab- bit all the carrots again."

229. Knock knock!

Who is there?

"Roo."

"Roo, who?"

"Roo are you?"

230. Knock knock!

Who is there?

"Winnie the."

"Winnie the, who?"

"Ha! You are silly. It is not Winnie the Who. It is Winnie the Pooh!"

231. Knock knock!

Who is there?

"Z."

"Z, who?"

"Z honey. Where is Z honey?!"

232. Knock knock!

Who is there?

"Alderaan."

"Alderann, who?"

"Alderaan the fastest mile in the race."

233. Knock knock!

Who is there?

"Art."

"Art, who?"

"R2-D2."

234. Knock knock!

Who is there?

"Ahsoka."

"Ahsoka, who?"

"Ahsoka my beans beans before I cook them. You do not?"

235. Knock knock!

Who is there?

"BB-8."

"BB-8, who?"

"BB-8 no one, I hope. That would be disgusting!"

236. Knock knock!

Who is there?

"Bespin."

"Bespin, who?"

"Bespin wins."

237. Knock knock!

Who is there?

"Boba Fett."

"Bobba Fett, who?"

"Bobba Fett my sandwich."

238. Knock knock!

Who is there?

"Beru."

"Beru, who?"

"You do not need to cry, it is not that bad of a Star Wars joke!"

239. Knock knock!

Who is there?

"Endor."

"Endor, who?"

"Is this the Endor the beginning of something great?"

240. Knock knock!

Who is there?

"Ewok."

"Ewok, who?"

"Ewok'd the door. Pwease wet me in!"

241. Knock knock!

Who is there?

"Kylo."

"Kylo, who?"

"Kylo, Kylo, it is off to work I go."

242. Knock knock!

Who is there?

"Leia."

"Leia, who?"

"Leia hand on me and I will make you hurt!"

243. Knock knock!

Who is there?

"Leia."

"Leia, who?"

"Can you Leia cookie on my plate please? I do not need any more veggies."

244. Knock knock!

Who is there?

"Luke."

"Luke, who?"

"Luke out! Here comes another joke!"

245. Knock knock!

Who is there?

"Ketchup."

"Ketchup, who?"

"Ketchup with me and I will tell you!"

246. Knock knock!

Who is there?

"Hank."

"Hank, who?"

"What are you hanking me for? I did not do anything!"

247. Knock knock!

Who is there?

"Foster."

"Foster, who?"

"He is Foster than a speeding bullet!"

248. Knock knock!

Who is there?

"Padme."

"Padme, who?"

"Padme down if you need to, but I need to come in now!"

249. Knock knock!

Who is there?

"Yoda."

"Yoda, who?"

"Yoda coolest kid!"

250. Knock knock!

Who is there?

"Watto."

"Watto, who?"

"Watto you want with me?"

251. Knock knock!

Who is there?

"Icy."

"Icy, who?"

"I see you!"

252. Knock knock!

Who is there?

"Ida."

"Ida, who?"

"No, it is Idaho!"

253. Knock knock!

Who is there?

"I do not know."

"I do not know, who?"

"Well, that is rude. I know you! You should know me."

254. Knock knock!

Who is there?

"Iguana."

"Iguana, who?"

"Iguana give you a hug. Get over here!"

255. Knock knock!

Who is there?

"Ike."

"Ike, who?"

"Ike ant stop laughing at all my great knock knock jokes!"

256. Knock knock!

Who is there?

"Ike."

"Ike, who?"

"Ike – ood have partied all night, but I needed to be responsible."

257. Knock knock!

Who is there?

"Ima."

"Ima, who?"

"Ima smart dad!"

258. Knock knock!

Who is there?

"Ina Claire."

"Ina Claire, who?"

"Ina Claire day you can see for miles and miles."

259. Knock knock!

Who is there?

"Doughnut."

"Doughnut, who?"

"Doughnut ask, it is a secret!"

260. Knock knock!

Who is there?

"Boo."

"Boo, who?"

"I did not mean to make you cry! It's just me!"

261. Knock knock!

Who is there?

"India."

"India, who?"

"India end, the good guys always win."

262. Knock knock!

Who is there?

"Gabe."

"Gabe, who?"

"I Gabe it my best shot, but it was not enough."

263. Knock knock!

Who is there?

"Gable."

"Gable, who?"

"Gable, Gable, Gable. Happy Thanksgiving, all!"

264. Knock knock!

Who is there?

"Garden."

"Garden, who?"

"Stop garden the door and let me in."

265. Knock knock!

Who is there?

"Gee."

"Gee, who?"

"Gee, I cannot remember the rest of this joke...."

266. Knock knock!

Who is there?

"Jenna."

"Jenna, who?"

"Do you know how to start the Jenna – rator? The power is out again."

267. Knock knock!

Who is there?

"Ghana."

"Ghana, who?"

"Ghana play with me now?"

268. Knock knock!

Who is there?

"Ghost."

"Ghost, who?"

"Ghost-and over in the corner. I am mad at you!"

269. Knock knock!

Who is there?

"Goat."

"Goat, who?"

"It is time to goat-oo bed!"

270. Knock knock!

Who is there?

"Goo."

"Goo, who?"

"Well, why not Google it?"

271. Knock knock!

Who is there?

"Goose."

"Goose, who?"

"It is time to goose 'E' your mother."

272. Knock knock!

Who is there?

"Handel."

"Handel, who?"

"Make sure you Handel with care! I am fragile!"

273. Knock knock!

Who is there?

"Gorilla."

"Gorilla, who?"

"Hey, can you gorilla me a hamburger or hot dog?"

274. Knock knock!

Who is there?

"Grant."

"Grant, who?"

"I will Grant you a wish if you let me in the house!"

275. Knock knock!

Who is there?

"Grape."

"Grape, who?"

"You are doing a grape job. Keep it up!"

276. Knock knock!

Who is there?

"Gravy."

"Gravy, who?"

"It is Gravy Crocket, the king of the wild frontier!"

277. Knock knock!

Who is there?

"Grimm."

"Grimm, who?"

"Just grimm and bear it, okay?"

278. Knock knock!

Who is there?

"Hammond."

"Hammond, who?"

"I would like Hammond eggs, please."

279. Knock knock!

Who is there?

"Claire."

"Claire, who?"

"Claire the way; I am coming in!"

280. Knock knock!

Who is there?

"Gus."

"Gus, who?"

"Who?"

281. Knock knock!

Who is there?

"Butter."

"Butter, who?"

"We butter get going."

282. Knock knock!

Who is there?

"Zany."

"Zany, who?"

"Zany idea where I put my glasses?"

283. Knock knock!

Who is there?

"Zap."

"Zap, who?"

"Zap you!" *Pretend to zap with your finger.*

284. Knock knock!

Who is there?

"Zax."

"Zax, who?"

"Thanks for coming! Zax all, folks!"

285. Knock knock!

Who is there?

"Zealous."

"Zealous, who?"

"Actually, zealous you know about who I am, the better."

286. Knock knock!

Who is there?

"Zinka."

"Zinka, who?"

"Zat iceberg zinka zhe boat."

287. Knock knock!

Who is there?

"Zit."

"Zit, who?"

"Zit time to open the door yet?"

288. Knock knock!

Who is there?

"Ziti."

"Ziti, who?"

"Ziti is for hitting zhe golf bar far."

289. Knock knock!

Who is there?

"Zombies."

"Zombies, who?"

"Zom-bees make honey, zom-bees do not."

290. Knock knock!

Who is there?

"Zoo."

"Zoo, who?"

"Zoo fly, do not bother me!"

291. Knock knock!

Who is there?

"Zoom."

"Zoom, who?"

"With zoom do you think you are talking to?"

292. Knock knock!

Who is there?

"Zzzzzz."

"Zzzzzz, who?"

"Zzzzzz. Hey, why did you wake me up? Did you not see that I was sleeping?"

293. Knock knock!

Who is there?

"D -1."

"D- 1, who?"

"I am D- 1 knocking at D-door. Let me in!"

294. Knock knock!

Who is there?

"Dancer."

"Dancer, who?"

"Well, dancer is that it is me knocking at your door."

295. Knock knock!

Who is there?

"Debbie."

"Debbie, who?"

"Debbie or not Debbie. That is the question."

296. Knock knock!

Who is there?

"Deduct."

"Deduct, who?"

"Daffy deduct."

297. Knock knock!

Who is there?

"Snow."

"Snow, who?"

"Snow body is home. Go away!"

298. Knock knock!

Who is there?

"Dyna."

"Dyna, who?"

"You are dyna-mite. Boom!"

299. Knock knock!

Who is there?

"Ear."

"Ear, who?"

"Ear you are, do you not nose how long I have been searching for you? Eye ready to go!"

300. Knock knock!

Who is there?

"East."

"East, who?"

"East too early to be up and speaking without coffee."

301. Knock knock!

Who is there?

"Eaton."

"Eaton, who?"

"I am Eaton my vegetables. Can I have cake now?"

302. Knock knock!

Who is there?

"Ed."

"Ed, who?"

"Ed-ucation is important, my son!"

303. Knock knock!

Who is there?

"Edwin."

"Edwin, who?"

"You know, Edwin this game if I just practiced more."

304. Knock knock!

Who is there?

"Egg."

"Egg, who?"

"This is egg-stremely boring out here. Can I please come in now?"

305. Knock knock!

Who is there?

"Edwin."

"Edwin, who?"

"Edwin some, I lose some."

306. Knock knock!

Who is there?

"Egypt."

"Egypt, who?"

"That man is a thief! Egypt me out of my money!"

307. Knock knock!

Who is there?

"Egypt."

"Egypt, who?"

"That man just punched me in the face! Egypt my front tooth!"

308. Knock knock!

Who is there?

"Fallon."

"Fallon, who?"

"Help! I Fallon, and I cannot get up!"

309. Knock knock!

Who is there?

"Fanny."

"Fanny, who?"

"Fanny you say that, I was just going to ask the same thing!"

310. Knock knock!

Who is there?

"Fanny."

"Fanny, who?"

"Fanny body calls tonight, make sure to tell them I am not home!"

311. Knock knock!

Who is there?

"Hallie."

"Hallie, who?"

"Hallie-tosis will make your breath stink, so make sure to brush your teeth!"

312. Knock knock!

Who is there?

"Farmer."

"Farmer, who?"

"Farmer answers to your questions you better let me in!"

313. Knock knock!

Who is there?

"Ha."

"Ha, who?"

"Ha Ha."

314. Knock knock!

Who is there?

"Haden."

"Haden, who?"

"Can we play Haden go seek?"

315. Knock knock!

Who is there?

"Hagen."

"Hagen, who?"

"Quit Hagen das joke book!"

316. Knock knock!

Who is there?

"Heffa."

"Heffa, who?"

"Heffa cookie is far better than none!"

317. Knock knock!

Who is there?

"Hair."

"Hair, who?"

"Hair today, gone tomorrow!"

318. Knock knock!

Who is there?

"Figs."

"Figs, who?"

"Figs that doorbell, it is broken!"

319. Knock knock!

Who is there?

"Hal."

"Hal, who?"

"Well, hallo there, little fellow! Hal are you doing today?"

320. Knock knock!

Who is there?

"Fanta."

"Fanta, who?"

"It is Fanta Clause! Ho, ho, ho!"

321. Knock knock!

Who is there?

"Grub."

"Grub, who?"

"Go ahead, grub my head for good lcuk."

322. Knock knock!

Who is there?

"Go dye."

"Go dye, who?"

"Go dye -rectly to jail. Do not pass go. Do not collect $200."

323. Knock knock!

Who is there?

"Obi Wan."

"Obi Wan, who?"

"Obi Wan a cracker?"

324. Knock knock!

Who is there?

"Gladys."

"Gladys, who?"

"Are you not Gladys finally the weekend?"

Chapter 5: Silly Stories

1. Kid says to dad, "I'm hungry." Dad says, "Oh, nice to meet you hungry." Kid says, "No, dad, I'm serious." Dad replies, "Oh, I thought you said you were hungry. Nice to meet you, serious." Kid says, "Are you kidding?" Dad says, "No, I'm dad!"

2. Kid says to dad, "Did you get a haircut?" Dad replies, "No, I got them all cut!"

3. Kid says to dad, "Can you put my shoes on?" Dad replies, "No, I do not think they will fit me!"

4. Kid says to dad, "Can I watch the TV?" Dad replies, "Yes, but make sure to turn it on."

5. Kid says to dad, "Ouch! I hurt myself!" Dad replies, "Oh! Well, the good news is that it will feel better when it stops hurting."

6. Kid says to dad, "I will call you later." Dad replies, "Please do not do that. I always have to remind you to call me dad!"

7. Cashier says to dad, "Do you want me to put the milk in the bag?" Dad replies, "No! Definitely not! Just leave it in the jug please."

8. Kid says to dad, "Hey! Make me a sandwich!" Dad replies, while waving a butter knife as a wand, "Poof! You are now a sandwich!"

9. Kid says to dad, "can you help me with my math homework?" Dad replies, "sure, why not start with this first problem?" Kid says to dad, "No, that one is a piece of cake." Dad replies, "No.... this is a math problem!"

10. Kid says to dad, "Hold up. I have something in my shoe." Dad replies, "Yep, you do. I'm pretty sure it is a foot."

11. Lady at the drive through window says to dad, "Any condiments?" Dad replies, "Compliments? Sure! You appear very lovely today!"

12. Kid says to dad, "Can you help me come up with a password? It needs to be eight characters long." Dad replies, "Sure, Show White and the Seven Dwarfs."

13. Kid says to dad, "What did you and mom do last night?" Dad replies, "Not much. We watched four movies back-to-back. Thankfully I was the one looking toward the TV!"

14. Kid says to dad, "Dad, can you tell me your absolute best joke ever?" Dad replies, "You."

15. Kid says to dad, "Where is the bin?" Dad replies, " I have not been anywhere!"

16. Kid says to dad, "Tell me about the time you fell in love with mom." Dad replies, "I fell in love during a back flip." Kid says, "What?" Dad says, "Yeah, I was heels over head for her!"

17. Kid says to dad, "I have to go to the hospital to see my friend." Dad replies, "Did you hear about the man who woke up there the other day and was freaked out because he could not feel his legs anymore?" Kid says, "No, I did not hear about it." Dad says, "Yeah, the doctor told him that it is good that he could not because he had amputated his arms!"

18. Kid says to dad, "What did you do last night?" Dad replies, "Your mom told me to take a spider out instead

of killing it. We went to the bar for a couple drinks. He is a cool dude. He wants to be a web designer!"

19. Kid says to dad, "How is the new job?" Dad replies, "Great. There are only two of us allowed to work on the Dracula figures on the toy production line. We have to make every second count."

20. Kid says to dad, "It is so muggy out today." Dad replies, "If I go outside and all our mugs are on the front lawn, you are in big trouble!"

21. Kid says to dad, "Why are you standing in front of that mirror?" Dad replies, "I am admiring my six pack. But I should hurry up and put them back into the fridge. I do not want them to get warm."

22. Kid says to dad, "What did you do last night?" Dad replies, "Well, your sisters hamster escaped from its cage. I spent four hours looking for it. No luck though. He definitely was not at the bar."

23. Doctor says to dad, "what brings you in today?" Dad replies, "I am worried. I think I have five legs!" Doctor says, "Oh my. Well, how do your pants fit?" Dad says,

"Like a glove!"

    a. Kid says to dad, "How are you and mom doing?" Dad replies, "Well, at breakfast this morning she told me she was leaving me. Said it was because I was obsessed with Twitter. I almost choked on my #toast!"

    b. Server says to dad, "Here is the check. Is there anything else I can get for you?" Dad replies, "Yeah, someone to pay for it!"

24. Kid says to dad, "Anything new?" Dad replies, "Well, I found out that I am color blind today. The news came right out of the gray!"

25. Kid says to dad, "There is a hole in my sock." Dad replies, "Mine too. That is how I get my foot in."

26. Doctor says to dad, "You only have about four months to live." Dad replies, "The hell I do!" and he shoots the doctor. Later the judge says to dad, "You are sentenced to 20 years to life." Dad replies, "Well, that is better!"

27. Friend says to dad, "You do not know the meaning of 'ironic.'" Dad replies, "Well, is that not ironic. We are at

a train station!"

28. Friend asks kid, "What does your dad do for a living?" Kid replies, "He is a magician. He performs tricks like sawing people in half." Friend says, "Do you have any siblings?" Kid replies, "Sure. I have four half-brothers and a half-sister."

29. Dad says to old friend with one arm, "Where you headed?" one-armed man replies, "To change a light bulb." Dad says, "Is that hard to do with one arm?" one-armed man replies, "I do not think it will be. I have the receipt."

30. Kids says to dad, "Do dads always snore?" Dad replies, "No. Just when we are sleeping!"

31. Kid says to dad, "Do you think corn is a good thing to grow in my garden this year?" Dad replies, " Yes! It is a maize-ing!"

32. Mom says to dad, "How am I looking?" Dad replies, "With your eyes, or course!"

33. Dad says to kid, "I think I broke my butt." Kid replies, "Why do you think that?" Dad says, "Because there is a

big crack in it!"

34. Kid says to dad, "Please do not sing those Oasis songs anymore." Dad replies, "Maayyyyybbbbbeeeeee!"

35. Kid says to dad, "I cannot find a warm spot in this house." Dad replies, "Try standing in the corner. It is 90 degrees there."

36. Dad says to the bookstore clerk, "Where is the self-help section?" The clerk replies, "If I told you that would be defeating the purpose."

37. Kid says to dad, "I am a chip off the ol' block!" Dad replies, "You kind of more like a peanut than a chip."

38. Airline attendant to dad, "Would you like to leave your bags?" Dad replies, "Absolutely!" But mom chimed in, "No, the kids need to come with us!"

39. Dad says to kid, "See that graveyard over there. Do you know why I cannot be buried there?" Kid replies, "No, why?" Dad says, "Because I am no dead yet!"

40. Kid says to dad, "What time is it?" Dad replies, "I have no idea. It keeps changing!"

41. Dad says to kid, "Have you eve noticed that geese fly in a 'V,' but one side is always longer than the other side?" Kid replies, "Yeah. Why is that?" Dad says, "Because there are more geese on that side."

42. Job interviewer says to dad, "What are your strengths?" Dad replies, "I fall in love easily." Interviewer says, "And what are your weaknesses?" Dad says, "Those blue eyes of yours."

43. Teacher says to the class, "The principal is coming to class today. I want to impress her." The class replies, "Okay, what can we do?" The teacher says, "When I ask a question, if you know the answer raise your right hand. If you do not, raise your left."

44. Petrol station worker calls dad and says, "Sir, you left something back at the gas station." Dad replies, "Really? I stopped there 30 miles back. What did I forget?" The station worker says, "Your wife." Dad says, "Oh! Thank god. I was worried I had gone deaf."

45. Dad says to the pet shop worker, "I want to buy a goldfish?" The worker replies, "Sure. Do you want an aquarium?" Dad says, "I really do not care what sign it is."

46. A man says to a lawyer, "How much do you charge?" The lawyer replies, "$1,000 for three questions." The man says, "Yikes! That is a little expensive is it not?" The lawyer says, "Yes. So what is your third question?"

47. Kid says to dad, "Hey dad, I have been thinking.... " Dad replies, "I though I smelled something on fire!"

48. Kid says to dad, "Are you alright?" Dad replies, "No, I am half left."

49. Doctor says to dad, "What is your blood type?" Dad replies, "Red."

50. Server says to dad, "My apologies regarding the wait." Dad replies, "Are you calling me fat?"

51. Kid says to dad, "Do you mind putting the dog out?" Dad replies, "I did not know it was on fire!"

52. "A jumper cable walked into a bar. The bartender says, 'I'll serve you, but do not start anything.'"

53. "A termite walks into a bar and asks, 'Is the bar tender here?'"

54. "A sandwich walks into a bar. The bartender says, 'Sorry, we do not serve food here.'"

55. "A man walks into a bar and asks for helicopter chips. The bartender replies, 'Sorry, we only have plane.'"

56. "A snake walks into the bar. The bartender says, 'Hey, how did you do that?'"

57. "Three blondes walk into a bar. You would think one would have seen it."

58. "A three-legged dog walks into a bar. He says to the bartender, 'I am looking for the man that shot my paw.'"

59. "The past, present, and future walked into a bar. Things suddenly got very tense."

60. "Three conspiracy theorists walked into a bar. There is no way you can tell me that it was a coincidence!"

61. "A duck walks into a pharmacy. He says to the clerk, 'Give me some chapstick. And this time put it on my bill."

62. "A bear walks into a restaurant. The server asks him what he wants and the bear says, 'I want a grilled .... cheese sandwich.' The server looked a little concerned and asked, 'Why did you pause?' The bear looks back angrily, 'What do you mean? I am a bear!'"

63. "A man was walking in a dessert with his dog and his horse. The dog finally stops and looks at the man. The dog then says, 'I cannot do this anymore. I nee water.' The man looked surprised and said, 'I had no idea dogs could talk!" The horse shakes its head and says, 'Me either!'"

64. "What stays out all night long and is Irish? Pati O. Furniture."

65. "Why did the turkey run across the road? Because it was not chicken."

66. "Where do people find chili beans? At the North Pole."

67. "You know, your grandparents always favored your uncle more than me, even though we are twins. It finally dawned on me when they asked me to blow up balloons for his surprise birthday party one year."

68. "The other day I was watching your nephews. We went and played a round of mini golf. Each kid kept fighting over who was winning. When some guy passing by asked who was coming in first, each one started shouting even louder. I just looked over and said, "Clearly their mother is..."

69. "Your sister wrote me a card with things I would never say in it. It included, 'Can you turn that up?' 'You can borrow my truck. Here is gas money.' 'Your new tattoo is awesome. Why don't we go get another one together?' and 'Here, you can be in charge of the remote.' I think she understands me."

70. "The day you get your driver's license is the day I finally get to sit in back and kick your seat!"

71. "I tried to impart some philosophical teaching to your sibling yesterday. While we were outside raking up leaves and getting the house ready we decided to take a little break. We rested on the stairs and looked up to

the sky. That was when Jenny asked, 'Why are we here?' I unloaded all my theories and learning about who we are as humans and all sorts of good spiritual stuff they talk about in church. Really went on in depth. I really thought I would have a major parenting win with this talk. I finally got to the end of my lecture and asked her if I answered her question. She said, 'Not really.' I was shocked! I tried to rack my brain for all sorts of other reasons we are here when she asked me again, 'Why are we here?' I was stumped. I just gaped back her with a stupid look on my face. That was when she chimed up again, 'We were supposed to pick mom up at the airport over an hour ago, right?'"

72. Advice other dads have given to their kids over the years:

    a. Columbus: "It does not matter what you discovered, son. You can still write your old man!"

    b. Michelangelo: "You know, normal children color on the walls. Do you have any idea how hard it is to get this stuff off the ceiling?"

c. Napoleon: "Ok, son. If you are not hiding something in your jacket, then pull your hands out of there and prove it to me."

d. Goldilocks: "Young lady, you have some explaining to do. Why do I have a bill here from the Bear family for a broken chair and a cleaning service?"

e. Einstein: "I understand that your hair is part of your statement, but these pictures are your senior portraits. Can you at least comb it or put some gel in there? Can you just do something?"

f. Edison: "Yes, son. I am very proud you came up with the electric light bulb. But now it is bed time and you need to turn that light out!"

g. Humpty Dumpty: "I have told you a thousand times not to sit on that wall. But no matter how many times or ways I have said it to you, do you think you listen to me? Of course not!"

73. The differences between dads today and dad's over 100 years ago:

a. 100 Years ago: Put a roof over you = success.

b. Today: Put a roof over you, a pool in the backyard, a three-car garage, and that is only for the vacation home = kind of doing well for the family.

c. 100 Years ago: hung out waiting to hear that the baby was born while smoking a cigar and drinking scotch.

d. Today: In the room trying to remember to switch the camera ot record mode, modeling the proper breathing technique, and being called a jerk.

e. 100 Years ago: Politely woke up the children to get them ready to go to school.

f. Today: Kids violently wake up dad to be driven to before-school sports practice.

g. 100 Years ago: Comes home to a family waiting to start a from-scratch dinner.

h. Today: Note taped to the fridge, 'Kids at practice. I am at gym. Leftovers in fridge. See you tomorrow?

74. "There were four fathers in the waiting room while their wives' were in labor. The first man received the great news from the nurse, 'Congratulations! You have twin boys!' The man replies, 'That is great! It is such a coincidence that I work for the Minneapolis Twins!' A few minutes later the nurse returns and tells the second man, 'Congratulations! You are now a father of triplets!' The second man got teary-eyed and replied, 'That is interesting. I work for the 3M Corporation!' Again, a few minutes later, the nurse returns to talk with the third man. She says, 'This is amazing! Your wife has given birth to quadruplets!' The man gets so excited he jumps up and says, 'Wow! I work for the Four Seasons Hotel. This is amazing!' At this news, the fourth man hits the floor, having fainted after hearing this interaction. The nurse is able to get him to come around and all of the father's and the nurse ask him what is wrong. The fourth man replies, 'What do you mean what is wrong?! I work for seven up!'

75. "Your uncle played a dangerous game the other day. He called up your cousins and told them that he was divorcing your aunt. He told them that over 40 years of marriage was enough and that he cannot take it any

more. He apologize that the news was being shared so close to the holidays but enough was enough. Of course your cousins freaked out and called each other to figure out what to do. Finally, your cousin Andy called your Uncle and screamed at him for a good 30 minutes. He went on and on, telling your uncle, 'Do not do a thing until we get there. My sister and I are on our way. Do not make any decisions until we arrive. Can you at least agree to that? We will be there before Thanksgiving.' Your uncle hung up and had a smug look on his face. He said, 'We did it! The children are visiting for Thanksgiving and they are paying for their own flights to visit us!'"

76. "I have come up with a list of the top things a dad never wants to hear on Father's Day:

   a. 'I love going through the motions of love and appreciation with you this time every year.'

   b. 'I realize you hate golf, but it was the easiest thing I could shoplift for you.'

   c. 'We are going to a restaurant for dinner, dad. This means you have to wear a shirt.'

d. 'The trimmer is not just for your nose. It is for your ear hair, too.'

e. 'I was thinking that today is a great day to make some updates to that will of yours.'

f. 'Are you serious? You expect me to give you a gift and celebrate you for ruining my life?'

g. 'You are our dad? I always thought of you like a second mother.'

h. 'Who are you?'"

77. "To celebrate Father's Day, a little boy got up early to make his dad breakfast. He cooked eggs and made toast and coffee. He brought it up to his dad in bed, and handed the food and drink to him. The dad take s a sip of the coffee and it is the strongest stuff he has ever tasted. Not wanting to hurt his son's feelings, he tells the boy that it is something. He says that he has never tasted coffee like that before. The boy beams with delight and tells his dad to drink more. As the dad continues to drink he sees a couple of soldier toys in the bottom. The dad looks puzzled and asks his son why there are little G.I. Joe's in his coffee. The boy breaks into song, 'The best part of waking up, is soldiers in

your cup!'"

78. "Your brother left me a note on his bed the other day. Scared the crap out of me. He had made his bed and straightened his room, so I knew right away something was wrong. The note said he was eloping with his girlfriend, the one we have never met. He knows we would not approve of her because of all the piercings and tattoos, apparently. Also, she is almost twice his age. She lives in a trailer in the woods and she has already chopped the wood to keep them warm through the winter. He wrote about all sorts of crazy things that they are going to do for money, especially since she was pregnant, too. At the very end of the note he wrote a little postscript. He said none of that other stuff was true, but that it was a reminder things could be a lot worse than the report card he had hidden in the middle drawer of his dresser. He also asked to be alerted when it was safe for him to come home. He is still out there somewhere."

79. "That picture of me holding you when you were just a few weeks old is my favorite. It showcases my prized possession. I wonder what ever happened to that golf shirt of mine."

80. "Several students came into class late during my exam. They claimed they had gotten a flat tire. Trying to be an understanding man, I told them that as long as all of them could answer one question correctly they would all get an 'A' on the test. They excitedly agreed and sat down for the question. I asked them, 'What tire was flat?'"

81. "I was driving on my way to work the other day and hit a duck that was flying very low to the ground. I guess that is one bird that does not live up to its name!"

82. "Your mom gave me the grocery list. I went to the store and brought the list. When I came home she started helping put away everything. She started getting more and more upset about the shopping I had done. She finally yelled, 'I cannot believe how bad you are at following a grocery list. I am never letting you do this again! You did not get anything on my list.' Guess I messed it up just enough to get out of doing that again!"

83. "Your sister had a sign posted on her door that read, 'I hate mom.' When I got home from work it was obvious that they had gotten into a fight and your mom was really upset. I decided to step in and be the hero. I

knew I could take care of this situation. I went into your sister's room and talked to her for a long time. When I came out I told your mother that she had nothing to worry about anymore. She no longer hated her. Of course, she changed the sign to say, 'I hate dad,' instead."

84. "Your mom ran out of gas the other day. I picked her up and we filled up a can at the gas station. When I drove her back to her car, I got out and filled up the car, using all the gas in the can. When I got back in the car, I told her she could get out and drive to the station to get more. She just looked at me and told me to drive both of us back to the station. Confused, I asked her why. 'Was one gallon not enough to get going again?' She just smiled and said, 'It would have been fine, had you put it in the right car.'"

85. "I noticed my sword collection was looking a little dusty. I left a note for the cleaning crew the next time they were scheduled to come saying, 'check my swords.' I came home expecting to find a gleaming display case but instead it looked just as dirty as before. Under my note was a new one that read, 'Nice swords.'"

86. "I was on my way to meet up with a client that drove me crazy. My face must have shown how unexcited I was because your little sister asked me what was wrong. I replied, 'I am on my way to meet a lady that loves to yell at your dad. She always makes me feel dumb.' Without missing a beat your sister replied, 'Oh! Well, tell mom I said hi!'"

87. "I see you left a note on your door to not disturb you because you were up late studying. I would like to take a moment to express management's thanks for staying with us, but it is important to remind you that checkout was at 11 AM ... when you turned 18.'"

88. "As your mom was unloading her suitcases for the trip here, I overheard another man say to his wife, who was also unloading her suitcases onto a cart to bring into the airport, 'Honey, I think you may have forgotten the kitchen sink!' I looked over at them instantly inserting myself saying, 'Do not worry. My wife remembered hers. The two of you can share.'"

89. "Your mom and I have had our fair share of battles over the years. Thankfully none of them ever amounted to very much. Sooner or later one of always realized that I

was wrong."

90. "I foolishly gave your mom a piano for her birthday this year. I finally convinced her to switch it out for a flute. This way she cannot sing along!"

91. "I was at the store the other day when a woman came rushing in, asking where the anniversary cards where. Clearly she was in trouble of being caught forgetting a special occasion. Before the clerk could reply I hollered out, 'The cards are over here, dear!' You should have seen the look on your mother's face when she saw me in the same aisle."

92. "Your mother made lasagna tonight. Make sure to lean over your plate so you get less on ya'!"

93. "Make sure not to yell through the screen door. You will strain your voice!"

94. "There is a reason that snakes never press themselves against their glass cages. They do not want to be windshield vipers!"

95. "I was bending over to tie a little boys shoes the other day. He gently rubbed my bald spot on the top of my

head and asked, 'You have a hole in your head! Does it hurt?' I continued tying the boys shoes and whispered in reply, 'Well, not physically.'"

96. "You know, if you ask me if I would do it all over again and have kids, I would say yes. Just not you kids."

97. "A horse walked into a bar. The bartender looked up and said, 'Why the long face?'"

98. "A mushroom walks into a bar. The bartender says, 'Hey! You are not allowed in here. We do not serve mushrooms.' Looking sad, the mushroom replies, 'Why not?! I am a fungi!'"

99. "It is pretty amazing that I never make errors. I thought I made one once, but I was wrong."

100. "Bacon and eggs walked into a bar. They order a drink and the bartender says to them, 'I am sorry, we do not serve breakfast here.'"

101. Kid stands still. Dad says, "You are running through the woods, you are running through the woods, you are running through the woods..." Dad waves arms around the kids head. Then dad says, 'Close your eyes!'

When the kid closes his or her eyes, dad smacks them on the forehead and yells, 'Tree!" The kids ask, 'What did you do that for?' The dad replies, 'Never close your eyes when you are running through the woods!'"

102.   "Two muffins were baking in the oven the other day. One muffin whined, 'My god, is it hot in here!' The second muffin looks horrified and screams, 'It is a talking muffin!'"

103.   "A conservative, moderate, and liberal walk into a bar. The bartender says, 'Hi Mitt. What are you having today?'"

104.   "To the man that sits in a wheel chair and managed to steal my camouflage jacket. You can hide but you cannot run!"

105.   "I never have gone to a shooting range before. Today I decided to give it a shot!"

106.   "I told the bartender that people hate bending over to get their drinks. He really needs to raise the bar." "A lady in line at the bank asked me if I could help her check my balance. She was not doing well. She fell

right over when I pushed her."

107.   "Thank God I am so good at sleeping. I can do it with my eyes closed."

108.   "A woman walked into the library. She asked the librarian where the books about paranoia were located. The librarian replied, 'look behind you.'"

109.   "If you look really closely you will see that all mirrors look like eyeballs."

110.   "Jim said to me the other day, 'What rhymes with orange?' I replied, 'No, it does not. Nothing rhymes with orange.'"

111.   "A blind man walked into the bar. And he walked into a table. And a chair..."

112.   "It is interesting that two parallel lines have so much in common. It really is a shame that they will never meet."

113.   "I am very upset. It appears someone added dirt in my garden bed. The plot thickens."

114.   "The pastor at church the other day read a passage where God spoke to Matthew. He said, "Matthew, come forth and you will receive live forever." Unfortunately, Matthew came in fifth and only got a convection oven.

115.   "I finally wrote that book about reverse psychology. You should not buy it!"

116.   "I enjoy the classic phrase, 'An apple a day keeps the doctor away.' But I have found that an apple a day will keep just about anyone away if you chuck it at them hard enough!"

117.   "Your mom was worried about her weight the other day. I eased her mind when I explained that the more she weighs the more difficult she would be to kidnap. I told her she needed to stay safe and eat that cake."

118.   "If two wrongs do not make a right, give three wrongs a try."

119.   "I am not a lazy dad. I am just on 'energy saving' mode."

120.   "I am not shy. I am just holding back how
awesome I am so I do not intimidate you!"

121.   "So sorry about all the mean and awful and
accurate things I said about you last night."

Bonus Chapter: Knock Knock Jokes

The following chapter is from another book written by me called "Knock Knock Jokes". I hope you like it. Enjoy!

Bonus Chapter 1: Food Knock Knock Jokes

1. Knock knock!

Who is there?

Egg.

Egg who?

Excited to see me?

2. Knock knock!

Who is there?

Ice cream.

Ice cream who?

I'll scream if you don't let me in.

3. Knock knock!

Who is there?

Broccoli.

Broccoli who?

Broccoli doesn't have a last name, silly.

4. Knock knock!

Who is there?

Egg.

Egg who?

Extremely disappointed you still don't recognize me.

5. Knock knock!

Who is there?

Mango.

Mango who?

Man, please let the visitor in.

6. Knock knock!

Who is there?

Lettuce.

Lettuce who?

Let us in, it's cold out here.

7. Knock knock!

Who is there?

Olive.

Olive who?

Olive you. Do you love me too?

8. Knock, knock!

Who is there?

Water.

Water who?

What are you doing? Just open the door.

9. Knock knock!

Who is there?Water.

Water who?

What a way to answer the door.

10. Knock knock!

Who is there?

Pasta.

Pasta who?

Pass the salt please.

11. Knock knock!

Who is there?

Butter.

Butter who?

Better be quick, I have to go to the bathroom.

12. Knock knock!

Who is there?

Pudding.

Pudding who?

Putting on your shoes before your trousers is a bad idea.

13. Knock knock!

Who is there?

Chicken.

Chicken who?

Check in your pockets if you can't find your keys.

14. Knock, knock!

Who is there?

Orange.

Orange who?

Orange you glad to see me?

15. Knock, knock!

Who is there?

Mayonnaise.

Mayonnaise who?

Mayonnaise have witnessed the goodness of our God.

16. Knock, knock!

Who is there?

Lettuce.

Lettuce who?

Let us in, it's really hot out here.

17. Knock, knock!

Who is there?

Lettuce.

Lettuce who?

Let us in and you'll find out.

18. Knock, knock!

Who is there?

Cookie.

Cookie who?

Cook went and now I have to prepare every food.

19. Knock knock!

Who is there?

Orange

Orange who?

Aren't you going to answer the door?

20.Knock knock!

Who is there?

Honeydew.

Honeydew who?

Honey do you know how great you look right now?

21. Knock knock!

Who is there?

Apple

Apple who?

I'll pull your hair.

22. Knock knock!

Who is there?

Orange

Orange who?

Aren't you ready? Because we're leaving.

23. Knock knock!

Who is there?

Butter

Butter who?

I better not tell you.

24. Knock, knock!

Who is there?

Butter.

Butter who?

Better say your line now.

25. Knock, knock!

Who is there?

Butter.

Butter who?

I better not tell you.

26. Knock, knock!

Who is there?

Loaf.

Loaf who?

I just don't like bread, I love it.

27. Knock, knock!

Who is there?

Buddha.

Buddha who?

Butter this slice of bread for me.

28. Knock, knock!

Who is there?

Bullet.

Bullet who?

Bull ate all the hay and now he's hungry.

29. Knock, knock!

Who is there?

Bean.

Bean who?

Been a while since I last saw you.

30. Knock knock!

Who is there?

Orange.

Orange who?

Aren't you glad this joke is over?

31. Knock, knock!

Who is there?

Orange.

Orange who?

Aren't you happy there is no school next week?

32. Knock, knock!

Who is there?

Orange.

Orange who?

Aren't you glad we are out of school?

33. Knock, Knock!

Who is there?

Ice cream!

Ice cream who?

I'll scream if you won't let me eat.

34. Knock, knock!

Who is there?

Ice Cream Soda.

Ice Cream Soda who?

I'll scream soda whole world will hear.

35. Knock, Knock!

Who is there?

Godiva!

Godiva who?

God I have a terrible headache, do you have a painkiller?

36. Knock, Knock!

Who is there?

Honeydew!

Honeydew who?

Honey do you love me?

37. Knock, Knock!

Who is there?

Figs.

Figs who?

Fix the doorbell, it's broken.

38. Knock, Knock!

Who is there?

Kiwi.

Kiwi who?

Can we go to the store?

39. Knock Knock!

Who is there?

Duncan.

Duncan who?

Don't count your chicks before they hatch.

40. Knock, Knock!

Who is there?

Eat.

Eat who?

Eat your veggies!

41. Knock, knock!

Who is there?

Peas.

Peas who?

Please pass the butter!

42. Knock, knock?

Who is there?

Turnip.

Turnip who?

Turn up the volume, it's my favorite song.

43. Knock, Knock!

Who is there?

Lettuce.

Lettuce who?

Let us go to the park.

44. Knock, Knock!

Who is there?

Beets!

Beets who?

Beats me. I thought you knew.

45. Knock, Knock!

Who is there?

Carrot.

Carrot who?

Carrot-e CHOP

46. Knock, knock!

Who is there?

Beef.

Beef who?

Before I freeze, open the door.

47. Knock, knock!

Who is there?

Apple.

Apple who?

Apple New Year.

48. Knock, knock!

Who is there?

Ginger.

Ginger who?

The Ginger Bread Man.

49. Knock, knock!

Who is there?

Honey bee.

Honey bee who?

Honey be a dear and get me some water.

50. Knock, knock!

Who is there?

Sultan

Sultan who?

Salt and pepper.

51. Knock, knock!

Who is there?

Banana

Banana who?

Banana split!

52. Knock knock!

Who is there?

Sweden

Sweden who?

Sweeten the tea.

53. Knock knock!

Who is there?

Banana.

Banana who?

54. Knock knock!

Who is there?

Orange.

Orange who?

Aren't you glad I didn't say banana?

55. Knock, knock!

Who is there?

Beef

Beef who?

Before I get frostbite, hand me something warm.

56. Knock, knock!

Who is there?

Figs

Figs who?

Fix the cooker, it's not working.

57. Knock knock!

Who is there?

Ketchup.

Ketchup who?

Catch up with us and we can plan.

58. Knock, knock!

Who is there?

Jelly

Jelly who?

Helicopter.

59. Knock, knock!

Who is there?

Olive

Olive who?

I live right next door to her.

60. Knock, knock!

Who is there?

Turnip

Turnip who?

Turn up the volume, I can't hear you.

61. Knock, knock!

Who is there?

Orange

Orange who?

Aren't you glad am here?

62. Knock, knock!

Who is there?

Doughnut.

Doughnut who?

Don't ask, it's my secret.

63. Knock, knock!

Who is there?

Banana.

Banana who?

Banana messages for me?

64. Knock knock!

Jam.

Jam who?

Jam mind, I'm trying to get in.

Bonus Chapter: Riddles, Brain Teasers and Trick Questions for Kids

The following chapters are from another book written by me called Riddles, Brain Teasers and Trick Questions for Kids. I hope you like them. Enjoy!

Bonus Chapter 2: Easy Riddles

Questions and Answers

1. Hmm, what belongs to you but is used by others way more than you?

Why, it's your name, of course!

2. Now, my mum is a cloud, my dad is the wind, the cool stream is my son, and the fruits of the land are my daughters. Do you know what I am?

The rain!

3. Here's a tricky one: What goes up a chimney when down, but can't go down a chimney when up?

An umbrella!

4. What could possibly have a bottom at the top of them?

Your legs!

5. What has lots and lots of holes but can still hold a lot of water?

A sponge, silly!

6. Can you tell me: What kinds of stones are never found in the ocean?

Ha-ha, stones that are dry.

7. Hmm, why is the Sun oh so bright?

Because it does its homework and always pays attention in class!

8. On a road to somewhere far, I came across a bridge. On that bridge was a man with a bundle of wood which was neither crooked nor straight. What kind of wood was it?

Sawdust!

9. The first woman is a grandmaster of love. The second woman is a grandmaster of invaluable gems. The third woman is a grandmaster of big sticks. The fourth woman is a grandmaster of shovels. Who are these women?

The queens in a pack of cards!

10. A father and his son were enjoying a lovely bike ride until they crashed. Now, two ambulances came and took them to two different hospitals. Now, the man's son was in the operating room when the doctor suddenly said, "I cannot possibly operate on you, you are my son!" Tell me how is this even possible?

Did you get it? The doctor was his mum!

11. The Livingston family is wealthy and lives in a large, circular home. One morning, Mr. Livingston wakes up to find a big stain of fig jam on his lovely white carpet. Realizing that

everyone had fig and toast that morning, he sets about asking everyone in the house what they were doing. Based on the excuses, can you tell who is lying? William said, "I was playing football in the driveway." Mrs. Livingston said, "I was cleaning the corners of the house. They were filthy!" The chef said, "I was preparing tonight's roast, sir." Who had the dodgiest excuse?

It was Mrs. Livingston. The Livingston home is round, so it has no corners!

12. One night, a pastry chef, a farmer, and a chandler go to a local inn. When they finish eating, four people pay. Tell me, who is the fourth person?

Was it night or knight? Because if it was knight, that would mean a knight, a butcher, a baker, and a candlestick maker went to the inn. That would make it four people!

13. Hmm, what instrument can you hear perfectly fine but can never see?

Ha-ha, it's your voice! Try singing!

14. A man was cleaning the window panes of a thirty-story building when his foot slipped off the rung and sent him tumbling. Thankfully, he didn't get hurt. How did he survive?

He was only standing on the second rung of the ladder. The ladder was on the ground floor!

15. I have keys, but I have no locks. I have space, but I have no room. You can enter but cannot go outside. Do you know what I am?

A keyboard!

16. One sunny Sunday, two fathers and two sons decide to go out for a day of fishing. All of them catch only one fish each. How is it possible that they only bring three fish home?

There were a total of three people on the fishing trip: A grandfather, a father, and a son!

17. Tuesday, Sam, and Peter went to a restaurant to eat dinner. After eating dinner, they paid the bill (with gratuity, because they were good people). But Sam and Peter were not the ones who ended up paying for the meal. Who paid?

Why, it was their friend, Tuesday!

18. What has four legs in the morning, two legs in the afternoon, and three legs late at night?

A person. As a toddler, you crawl on your legs, as a grown-up, you walk on two, and when you're older, you walk with a walking stick, which makes it three legs.

19. If you use yellow bricks to build a yellow house, red bricks to build a red house, and blue bricks to build a blue house, then what, is a greenhouse made of?

Glass, silly!

20. A house has four walls. All of the walls are somehow facing south, and a big bear is circling the house, sniffing after a meal. What color is the bear?

Since the house is on the North Pole (an igloo, to be specific), that would make the bear a polar bear, which means it is white!

21. What is lighter than a feather, but can't be held for more than a few minutes?

His breath!

22. In a one-story red house, there was a red person, a red cat, a red fish, a red computer, a red chair, a red table, a red telephone, a red shower– everything was red! What color were the stairs?

There are no stairs; it's a one-story house!

23. A man was driving his truck. His lights were not on. The moon was not out. Up ahead, another man was crossing the street. How did the driver see him?

It was a bright and sunny day!

24. What has a head but never cries, has a bed but never sleeps, can run but doesn't walk, and has a bank but no money?

A river!

25. A boy leaves home, turning left precisely three times. When he gets back home, he is facing two masked men. Who are they?

A catcher and an umpire!

Bonus Chapter 3: More Easy Riddles

Questions and Answers

1. Pay close attention now. See, there are three houses in a row. One is a bright red, one is a dull blue, and one is a pearly white. If the bright red house is just to the left of the house in the middle, and the dull blue house is just to the right to the house in the middle, can you tell me where the white house is?

In Washington, D.C., of course!

2. You are in a small cabin, and it is pitch black. You have one match on you. Which do you light first, the day-old newspaper, the antique lamp, the stubby candle, or the fire?

Well, the first thing you should do is light the match!

3. Who is bigger in this family: Mr. Bigger, Mrs. Bigger, or their little baby son?

The baby, of course, because he is a little bigger.

4. Mike is a butcher. He is 5'10" tall and very wide at the shoulders. His boots are very heavy and so is his leather apron. What does he weigh?

He weighs meat.

5. A farmer has seventeen fluffy sheep and, after a great

disaster, all but nine die. How many are left?

Nine.

6. How far can a bunny run into the woods?

Halfway. You see, after that, he is running out of the woods.

7. In a year, there are twelve months. Seven months have 31 days. Keeping that in mind, how many months have 28 days?

They all do.

8. What are the next three letters in this sequence: J, F, M, A, M, J, J, A, ___, ___, ___?

S, O, N. You see, the given sequence has the first letters of the months of the year. September, October, and November are the next months in the sequence.

9. Jimmy's mum had four kids. She named the first one Monday. She named the second Tuesday, and she named the third Wednesday. What is the name of the fourth child?

Jimmy. Why? Because Jimmy's mum had four children!

10. Before Mt. Everest was famously discovered, what was the highest mountain in the world?

You guessed it, Mt. Everest. After all, it was still the highest in the world. It just had not been discovered yet!

11. Which is heavier between these two? A pound of feathers or a pound of rocks?

Neither. Both weigh one pound each!

12. What can hold water even though it is riddled with holes?

A sponge

13. A family lives in a large apartment building, 10 stories high. Each day, their son takes the lift from the family's apartment on the 10th floor to the lobby and goes off on his way to school. When he comes back in the afternoon, he uses the lift again to get to the 5th floor, and then uses the stairs for the remaining five floors. Why?

Because the son can't reach the buttons higher than five!

14. A plane crashes on the border of the United States and Canada. Where are the survivors buried?

You do not bury the SURVIVORS!

15. I don't have any superpowers, but I can predict the score of any basketball game before it begins. Can you tell me how I do this?

Well, that's easy – the score before any football game is always zero to zero!

16. You are driving a big, 20-seater bus. At the first stop, two

women get on. Pay attention. At the second stop, three men get on, and one woman gets off. Now we're at the third stop, three kids and their mum get on, and a man gets off. The bus is a cool grey color, and it is raining very heavily outside. Tell me the color of the bus driver's hair?

Whatever color your hair is! Don't forget, you're the bus driver!

17. Give me water, and I will die, give me food and I will live. Do you know what I am?

Fire.

18. Which travels faster, the heat or the cold?

The heat! You can catch a cold.

19. The moment you have me, you feel like sharing me. But, if you are foolish enough to share me, you do not have me anymore. Do you know what I am?

A secret.

20. What can you hold without ever touching with your hands?

Your breath, silly!

21. First, I threw away the outside and cooked the inside. Then I ate the delicious, delectable, delightful outside and threw

away the inside. What did I eat?

Corn on the cob.

Conclusion

Thank for making it through to the end of *2,000 Dad Jokes* let's hope it was enjoyable and able to provide you with all of the chuckles you need to make it through your day.

The next step in the process is to find those that made you laugh, that you enjoyed, and felt were relevant to your life and start repeating them over and over. Start by telling the jokes to yourself so many times you get sick of hearing yourself, and then start trying them out on the ones that you love. They are more likely to stick around for the long haul as you refine your dad-joke telling skills. Tell them over and over when the opportunity arises. Practice your timing and voice. Once you have practiced your skills on those that love you and you have all the delivery points down, you are ready to take them to the streets. They are ready for the world to hear. Throw one out at the next dinner party or PTA meeting. Offer up a little relief during a stressful work meeting or the next time you meet someone new.

A dad joke is more than just a cheesy one-liner or funny play on words. It is more than just a story that has a silly ending or message. It evokes the memory of father's past; of a simpler time. And it offers up a little chuckle that you can pass on to generations to come, like it has been passed on to you.

Finally, if you found this book useful in any way, a review on Amazon is always appreciated!

Printed in the USA
CPSIA information can be obtained
at www.ICGtesting.com
LVHW090852251123
764789LV00006B/1097